STORY CRAFTING

The Art of Preparing and Telling Stories

Jackson Day

STORY CRAFTING

The Art of Preparing and Telling Stories

Jackson Day

Story Crafting

THE ART OF PREPARING AND TELLING STORIES

Jackson Day

Opelika, Alabama 36803

Cover prepared by Erika Falcão

Layout prepared by José Gomes da Silva Neto

jackday@pobox.com

ISBN 978-0-9797324-3-0

Copyright © 2010 by Jackson Day, Opelika, AL. Permission is granted to use up to five pages of this document for non-commercial purposes provided the words "*Story Crafting* © *Jackson Day 2010,*" are included on all pages containing material from the document. Written permission is required for all commercial uses.

Story Crafting

ART OF STORYTELLING

	Page
Acknowledgments	7
My Storytelling Journey	11
No Formula Exists for Becoming a Storyteller	14
Storytelling Defined	15
Classifications of Storytellers	16
Sources of Stories	19
Record and Keep Story Ideas	23
Fiction or Reality	25
Structure of the Story	27
Crafting a Story	29
Key-character Information Form	33
Revising the Crafted Story	51
Reorganizing Your Crafted Story for Telling	56
Telling an Existing Story	63
Analyzing an Existing Story	65
Elements Used to Communicate the Story	68
Preparing to Tell the Story	78
Character Perspective Chart	79
Warm-up Before Storytelling	89

Listening Improves Storytelling 99
Children and Storytelling 104
Audience Participation 114
Categories of Stories 118
Suggested Reading 123
    Finding Stories to Tell in Your Public Library 123
    Books on Storytelling 125

Story Crafting

ACKNOWLEDGMENTS

A writer doesn't write alone and a storyteller must have listeners. Living with other people gives the storyteller stories and story-ideas. If I acknowledged all the people who have helped me as a storyteller, the acknowledgments would require more pages than the book.

I acknowledge that I was privileged to grow up in a farming community where my father's family frequently gathered on my grandparent's front porch to visit and swap stories. I was privileged to hear farm workers tell anecdotes and stories as they worked and when they relaxed.

I acknowledge that I can read and write because of my teachers. I have fond memories of most of my teachers. I feel a special debt to Mrs. Jo Ann Vann Cannon, who was my eleventh grade English and Speech teacher at Enterprise High School in Alabama. She told me that I had unique communication skills. She encouraged me to develop my communication skills, but advised me to work on improving grammar and spelling skills. She praised my strengths while challenging me to work on my weaknesses. In contrast, my twelfth grade English teacher told me that I had no writing skills and that I didn't have the mental capacity to do university work. Mrs. Cannon's encouragement helped me make a liar out of my twelfth grade English teacher.

I acknowledge that when I was studying at Samford University, I resented that I needed to work 40 plus hours a week in a barber shop to pay for my schooling while most students had parents who paid their bills. But looking through the rear-view mirror of life, I acknowledge that I was privileged to work as a barber. Storytelling barbers are the ones with the most customers, and I worked with some good storytellers. I gained more storytelling skills and people-skills in barber shops than in classrooms.

When I was in graduate school, I wrote homework papers in long hand and paid someone fifty cents a page to type them, before turning them in to professors. Once I asked a fellow student, who worked part time as a secretary, to type a paper for me. She refused payment. Her roommate suggested I express my thanks by taking her out to dinner. Ever since that "thank you" date, I've been unable to come up with ways to express my thanks for all the ways that woman has helped me. I acknowledge that my wife, Doris Day, has helped me more than anyone else. Sometimes she supports me, sometimes she leads me, but at all times she is my partner and best friend. I'm privileged to be married to the woman I love. I'm privileged that she shares my interest in storytelling. My wife has sharp eyes that catch spelling and grammar mistakes. I'm thankful that she's stern when correcting my writing mistakes, but she's gentle when correcting my other mistakes.

I acknowledge that Lyn Caudle was the first person to read my first draft of this book. His suggestions resulted in a lot of rewriting. Then fellow storyteller, Mrs. Giggs Couch, gave me her opinion of the book's weaknesses and suggested that I add anecdotes and concrete examples to illustrate my suggestions. Her advice resulted in further rewriting and additions.

I acknowledge that while living in Brazil for 33 years, I struggled to think and write in Portuguese. As a result, my English suffered. Portuguese is a phonetic language and words are spelled the way they sound. Sometimes I spell an English word phonetically and come up with a word that's not the one I need. Sometimes I use a Portuguese word as though it were an English one. One of my sons told me, "Daddy, you use Portuguese words as though they were English words, but you say them with such authority that everyone thinks you know what you are talking about." I acknowledge that I have a writer's blind spot. I see what I think I wrote instead of what

Story Crafting

I actually wrote. I asked several friends to read my book in progress, correct mistakes, mark what was confusing, and give suggestions for improving. Those who helped me are:

- Mrs. Ann Rice is a retired elementary school teacher. She used storytelling in her classroom and has performed as a storyteller in schools.
- Jeff Holley has taken two Bible storytelling training events with me and I have the privilege of coaching him as a Bible storyteller.
- Mrs. Jennifer Farris helped her husband get good grades in graduate school by editing his assignments. Her husband still depends on her to edit his writings. Jennifer is a stay at home mother with two preschool children. In her spare time, Jennifer is also a writer.

Story Crafting

MY STORYTELLING JOURNEY

Storytelling was a part of my childhood. I was raised on a farm near LaFayette, Alabama. Our family didn't have TV until I was twelve years old. On Sundays, my father's family went to our grandparents' house and sat on the front porch visiting. Visiting always included swapping stories. My grandparents were born shortly after the Civil War and would tell stories about the hard times following the Civil War. Uncle Sam would get us laughing with tales about stubborn milk cows. He would embellish on the doings of his neighbors; he told stories about his Collie fetching cows when it was milking time, and his dog protecting his grandchildren. Uncle Arlee was an auctioneer, and he would tell the latest jokes he heard at cattle sales. We had no TV, when neighbors or family went visiting, they entertained each other by telling stories.

LaFayette is in the Black Belt, so called because the rich black soil produced bumper crops when "Cotton was King" of the South. I grew up before the Civil Rights Movement. Black families were a majority in our community, and they were our closest neighbors and my good friends. On rainy days, I would visit Black neighbors and listen to their stories. I worked in the fields with Black workers hoeing weeds, picking cotton, gathering corn and mending fences. I'd hear Blacks tell stories as we worked. Black neighbors took me to a storyland full of delightful tales, talking animals, rhymes, jingles, and superstitions. Br'er Rabbit was "bred and born in the briar patch." I was bred and born in a community of Black storytellers.

I had to pay for my own university education. I heard someone mention a recent graduate who worked his way through university as a barber. I said, "I can do that." I bought barber tools and started cutting hair in a dorm bathroom at Samford University, Birmingham, Alabama. I am indebted to Coach Bobby Bowden, the football coach at Samford. Coach Bowden required every football player to have a crewcut, and he inspected their haircuts every Friday. Most of the players came to me for their haircuts on Thursday nights. They paid me a dollar for a haircut instead of paying a $1.50 at a barber shop.

I passed the test with the Jefferson County Barber Commission to become a licensed barber and went to work for Jimmy Williams, a storytelling barber in Mountain Brook. A customer would tell Jimmy about something. Jimmy would embellish the event and turn it into a story. He was always crafting new stories. Every time he repeated a story, he would improve it. Customers often stayed in the barber shop for hours after getting a haircut, listening to Jimmy tell stories.

I went to graduate school in Texas and worked in the Fort Worth Hotel Barber Shop. It was the first barber shop in Fort Worth that did men's hair styling. Many of our customers were CEO's, artists, musicians and politicians. My boss, Mr. Banks, came to work wearing a suit, hat and boots. He invested in paintings of young, talented artists with the hope that they would become famous and their paintings valuable. I went to my classes in the mornings and worked in the afternoons. Mr. Banks got his stories from different magazines. He would get a story from **Guideposts** to tell church-going customers and a story from **Playboy** for non-church-going customers. He would have about four different stories that he would continually repeat. He repeated the same stories for a couple of weeks, dropped them and picked up new ones. We, the employees, would hear the same story told with almost the same words more than 30 times, but customers would hear it only once.

I noticed that storytelling barbers were the ones with the most customers; so I was motivated to find and tell stories. I learned more about getting along with people and telling stories in the barber shop than in university or graduate school.

Story Crafting

My wife and I went to Brazil to teach the Bible and plant new churches. In Brazil, I learned the importance of telling Bible stories when I was teaching and preaching. When I was teaching or preaching from a part of the Bible that was not in story form, I tried to find stories from the Brazilian culture to illustrate each biblical teaching. I read Brazilian folk tales to help me understand the Brazilian culture.

Brazilians are great storytellers. I have fond memories of swapping stories with Brazilian friends. Most Brazilians turn the TV off when company comes, and they love to visit and receive visitors. Visiting always includes swapping stories. Living among storytelling Brazilians for 33 years gave me stories to tell and inspired me to find and share stories with others. The art of storytelling is best learned by listening to stories and telling stories. Living in the Brazilian storytelling culture, helped my storytelling abilities.

My wife and I returned to the USA in 2002.

After reaching retirement age, I went back to graduate school and studied storytelling performances at East Tennessee State University. I spent a week at Celebration Barn in South Paris, Maine, studying the Art of Storytelling with Milbre Burch and Antonio Rocha.

My wife and I continue to work at improving our storytelling abilities. We are always looking for opportunities to tell stories or to teach others to tell stories.

Story Crafting

NO FORMULA EXISTS FOR BECOMING A STORYTELLER

This is a book about the art of crafting and telling stories; however, storytelling is best learned by listening to stories, and then telling stories. No one has come up with a set of rules, or formula, or system, that tells someone how to become a good storyteller. If three rules exist for becoming a storyteller, nobody knows what they are. You can find some principles that seek to set in concrete aspects of storytelling; however, you will find good storytellers who intentionally and successfully break every one of those rules.

You can go to a university and study storytelling. While there, you will learn that many of the best known storytellers never studied storytelling; many didn't even finish high school. They grew up in a storytelling environment and they learned by listening and then telling stories.

This book is an attempt to share with others some of the things I have learned from listening to storytellers, telling stories, studying storytelling, and reading about storytelling.

Story Crafting

STORYTELLING DEFINED

Storytelling has three essential components: a story, a teller, and listeners. Storytelling is the narration through voice and gestures of an account of imaginary or real people and events to one or more listeners. Storytelling requires a face-to-face interaction between the storyteller and the story-listeners.

The process of storytelling starts in the imagination of the teller, moves through the verbal expressions of the teller, and ends up being experienced in the imagination of each listener. In order to move the experience from the storyteller's head to his listeners' imagination, the storyteller uses everything he has – his face, body, voice, sounds and words. The storyteller creates a world, whether it's a home, a school, a playground, a swimming pool, an airplane, a forest, a kitchen, a ball field or a battle field, that his listeners can inhabit instantly.

The need to share a story is the beginning of a storyteller. A storyteller is a person who has empathy for a story and a desire to touch his story-listeners. He does not just tell a story, he shares it with his listeners.

Story Crafting

CLASSIFICATIONS OF STORYTELLERS

I classify storytellers into three categories: casual storytellers, community storytellers and performing storytellers. These categories do not imply which are the best storytellers; but, they describe the situations in which they do their storytelling. One is not more important than another. Each is different; so it is helpful to distinguish between them. Excellent storytellers are in each category.

Storytellers are similar to musicians. Some people sing in the shower and when they are sitting in a church pew; some people sing in a church or community choir and are often invited to sing as volunteers at community events; some musicians are performers who volunteer to sing for special occasions; while other performers are paid to sing at concerts and for TV.

1. Casual storytellers

Casual storytellers automatically look for opportunities to spin a yarn. Most don't think of themselves as storytellers; they enjoy visiting and having fun with family and friends. They tell stories through the routine course of their lives. Their stories are usually spontaneous, seldom planned. Storytelling is woven into the fabric of their normal communications. They don't organize their stories into a text, nor do they practice or work on refining their style or voices.

Casual storytellers include the parent who entertains his children, the auto mechanic spinning a tale to a customer, the relative who entertains family members at family gatherings, the hunter and fisherman who tell tall tales, the camper who builds a bonfire and hopes somebody drops by to visit, men who regularly gather at a local café and sit at the "liar's table," and the co-worker who usually has a story to tell at coffee break.

2. **Community storytellers**

Community storytellers tell stories to share, teach, mold character, gain customers, and pursue clients. They usually do their storytelling within a professional or volunteer activity. Most have a profession or do activities that give them a platform to speak to people in their community, and they use storytelling as part of those activities. They don't consider themselves storytellers, but they weave storytelling into their jobs and volunteer activities. Their local community enjoys listening to their stories. They often plan their stories and work on improving both their stories and the telling of their stories.

Many barbers, beauticians and salesmen realize that storytellers attract customers like magnets attract iron; so they are on the lookout for something that they can embellish into a story. Many lawyers use storytelling to pursue clients or jurors. Many teachers, preachers, church Bible teachers, writers, and occasional public speakers become known in their local community as good speakers who use stories in their presentations.

3. **Performing storytellers**

Performing storytellers deliver stories to audiences who have gathered for the purpose of listening to stories. Their audiences expect the storytellers to be prepared artists who will present polished, rehearsed performances.

Some storytelling performers are volunteers, such as scout leaders who gather boy or girl scouts around a fire and tell stories, or volunteers who tell stories at children's hospitals or at retirement villages. Some storytellers have jobs that require them to perform, such as the librarian who does story time with children, or the park ranger who tells historical stories to tourists.

Some performing storytellers are professionals who are paid to entertain audiences with stories. Most are part-time professionals. They are retired or they combine storytelling with some other career, such as teaching, journalism or farming; and they receive invitations to do a few paid storytelling performances every year. But some storytellers make a living as storytelling performers; storytelling is their sole activity for earning money.

Story Crafting

SOURCES FOR STORIES

The storyteller can find many seed-beds with ideas for stories. I'm going to mention some of the sources where the teller can look for story seed-beds.

1. Personal experiences

Every person who survived his childhood has many stories stored in his memory to tell. Stories that grow out of a storyteller's experience have a powerful impact. Getting sick, breaking a bone, going to a doctor, getting lost, losing a friend, gaining a new friend, or moving to a new home are all personal experiences.

Personal stories may be the literal truth or they may be events that have been embellished for the sake of a story. Embellished stories may be rearranged and people's names changed in order not to embarrass them. Embellished stories may have several different real characters woven into one story character; different events over a period of several years may be woven into a time-frame of a day or a week.

2. Family stories

Almost every family has stories that are told when the relatives gather. They are stories of the doings of certain family members or events that happened to them. These stories help a family define their identity. Older family members often recount adventures of their formative years and of past generations. Older relatives are the best source for family stories which are usually about people, places or events.

Recall stories told by your parents and grandparents. Recall stories about you and your parents. Recall some of the things you did with your siblings and other family members. If you are married, you have some stories to tell about your mate, children and in-laws.

3. **Personal relationships**

Every personal relationship is a seed-bed for one or more stories. Boyfriend with girlfriend, husband with wife, friend with friend, boss with employee, co-worker with co-worker, and enemies are sources of many stories.

4. **Animals and pets**

Good stories can be found in animals that are or once were a part of your life.

5. **Places**

Places where a person lived, visited, worked, vacationed, studied or had contact with are a seed-bed that can sprout interesting stories. Places where parents and grandparents lived and worked, and told you about can be a seed-bed for a story. Places that are important to you are seed-beds to great stories.

Your personal geography can be explored for stories. You have contact with many different places. Consider the rooms in your house, the roads you drive, the stores you frequent, the trail you walk or jog, the place where you work, or the place where you go to relax.

6. **Significant life events**

Any significant happening has at least one story behind it. Starting school, birthdays, holidays, moving, graduating, getting married, death of a loved one, an accident or sickness of a family member are all significant life events.

Story Crafting

7. School

First day of school, best or worst year at school, good or bad teacher, bully, unusual student, making or not making the team, rivalry with fellow students, conflict with a teacher, graduating from school, and enrolling in a new school are all sources of good stories.

8. Trips

A vacation, a trip to visit friends or family, an excursion with friends, a business trip, or a trip to a distant and strange place are all sources of interesting stories. A drive in a car, an airplane flight, or an ocean voyage can be a seed-bed for several stories.

9. Secrets

Secrets hidden from others at a significant time in your life would catch the interest of others.

10. Crisis experiences

Failing a grade in school, getting fired, experiencing the death of a loved one, getting arrested, being responsible for losing a game, dealing with a child's arrest, or dealing with a child who is addicted to drugs are crisis experiences. Crisis experiences catch listeners' attention quicker than good experiences.

11. Embarrassing events

Examples of embarrassing events:

- Forgetting an appointment
- Knocking a dish over, falling over something, or dropping things at a formal dinner
- Being unaware that you were to speak at a meeting until you entered the door and received a bulletin that listed you as the key-speaker

- Being advised to dress casually for a meeting, you showed up in Bermuda shorts. However, all the other men showed up wearing casual dress pants, sport jackets and ties
- Finding your name on the front page of the newspaper, because a person whose name is the same as yours has committed a crime

Embarrassing events are sources of interesting and humorous stories.

12. Experiences in learning a new skill

Many examples can be found about learning a new skill, such as swimming, milking a cow, cooking, dancing, playing a musical instrument or driving a car. A new job often requires learning new work skills such as barbering, carpentering, sewing, cooking, etc. Often students and employees are required to learn to use new computer programs. These are all seed-beds for stories.

13. Hobbies

Hobbies that interest you or people you know can become sources of exciting stories.

14. Cross-cultural experiences

Cross-cultural experiences include living among people whose culture differs from your own, or relating to people from another culture who live within your culture are sources for interesting stories.

15. Literature

Literature can be a source of stories to tell. In literature, the storyteller finds stories written by someone else for the purpose of publication. Remember to respect copyright laws when telling a published story.

Literature can also provide the storyteller with seed-ideas for crafting original stories.

Story Crafting

RECORD AND KEEP STORY IDEAS

The storyteller needs to acquire the habit of writing down story ideas and keeping them in a safe place.

Stories come from many sources. However, if the storyteller does not record and keep story ideas, he will forget most of them. Some storytellers have a Story Notebook where they record and keep story ideas. I always have 3X5 note cards in my shirt pocket so I can jot down story ideas and later record them in my computer.

The important thing is to have a system for recording and keeping story ideas. The storyteller should record and keep notes on what he experiences, sees, hears and feels; and ideas about using them in a story. If something interests him, it has the seed for a story that will interest others.

There are no insignificant people, events, places, jobs or conversations for the storyteller. All have the potential for inspiring an interesting story. Most ideas in their infancy are flawed, silly or ridiculous. However, they still are story-seeds that can grow into powerful stories. So, if it catches your attention, make a note of it.

One of the best ways to find stories is simple observation. Observe an interesting person, event, place, object, situation or conversation. Then make notes about what you observed. Your notes become seeds that one day may grow into a story worth telling.

Often several years pass between the time I note a story-idea and the time when I finally craft the idea into a story. I wonder how

Record and Keep Story Ideas

many story-ideas were lost because I did not write them down and keep them for future reference.

Story Crafting

FICTION OR REALITY

1. **Reality**

    Real life situations are seed-beds for stories that make a powerful impact. Everyone has many stories to tell from his personal experiences. As a result, the storyteller can honestly tell about many events in his life. Also, the storyteller can tell true stories that happened to other people. The storyteller can craft stories from historical events.

2. **Fiction**

    Often, the storyteller does not want the truth to get in the way of a good story. When this happens, the storyteller can create fiction by reinventing the people and situations. Fiction inspired by reality results in believable stories.

    Many stories need to be told; however, naming people while telling the facts could anger the guilty or embarrass the innocent. If you would like to tell a story about a person, but not with him present, then don't tell it. Some stories are too sensitive to be told as history. For example, a story about an uncle celebrating the purchase of a new car by getting drunk and washing his new car with all the windows down could embarrass him, his children and grandchildren. Nevertheless, the story could be reinvented, placed in another location with characters who have different names, and told as fiction. Fictionalizing historical events with the substitution of fictional names for that of real people and locations avoid the risk of embarrassing people.

    Historical details may need to be filled with imagination because of incomplete knowledge or faded memory. When that happens, use the fragment that can be verified, invent the rest, make some adaptions and craft the story as a fiction.

Different situations that several people faced can be adapted into a crafted story so that one character faces them all.

Story Crafting

STRUCTURE OF THE STORY

A story must have a beginning, a middle, and an end. The beginning gets your listeners interested in the tale; the middle must keep them interested; the ending justifies the time they spent listening to the story.

The typical story adheres to the following structure:

Beginning:
- The initial-situation establishes the background by introducing the key-character(s) who lives in a clearly described time and place.
- The initial-problem is an inciting event that identifies a problem or need, and hints that trouble is on the way.

Middle:
- The sequence of events develops the core of the story with problem situations, progressive complications, conflicts, dialogues, outside interference, and aborted attempts at resolution.

Ending:
- The final-situation clarifies the outcome of the story.

Structure of the Story

SIMPLIFIED STRUCTURE OF A STORY	
BEGINNING	Initial-situation
	Initial-problem
MIDDLE	Sequence of events
ENDING	Final-situation

Story Crafting

CRAFTING A STORY

The beginner storyteller should be aware of the guidelines for crafting a story and follow them. The experienced storyteller may discover other effective ways of crafting stories. The following guidelines will help beginner storytellers craft stories for telling. They will also help the experienced storyteller improve storytelling skills. I've been telling stories for many years and I usually follow these guidelines when I am crafting a new story.

1. **Choose the key-character(s)**

    List the key-character(s) of the story.

    Next, list all the characters who are mentioned in the initial-situation. Then list other characters who will be added during the telling of the story.

    Characters are at the core of every story. Determine who are the key-character(s). In most stories, the key-characters will be people. However, key-characters may be non-humans, such as animals, plants or objects that are given people-like characteristics. Some stories only have one key-character; in others, more than one character stand out.

    A story for telling should not have more than three key-characters. Listeners have difficulty following a story with more than three characters.

    Principal characters should have names; however, minor characters may be designated by a status, role, or relationship. Examples would be: king, judge, neighbor, boss, teacher, or step-sister. This is characteristic of folktales and many Bible stories. For example, in the Bible story of the flood, Noah and his sons' names are mentioned; however, Noah's wife and daughter-in-laws go unnamed.

Organize the story around characters. Characters act, experience conflict and undertake struggles. The events in the story are generated by the key-character's predicament. If the storyteller doesn't create believable characters, listeners won't care what happens to them. Your task as a storyteller is to make your listeners see, hear, smell, and feel the key-character(s).

Wounded characters make for interesting stories. People desire to be rich, healthy, strong, and good looking. Such characters make for dull stories. A poor, sickly, weakly, ugly character makes a more interesting story. Here are some samples of different types of wounds:

- **Physical wound**: Allen was a football quarterback until his right arm was amputated in a motorcycle accident.
- **Social wound**: Sally was an intelligent, beautiful young lady. But she had no friends at school, because her parents were in jail for drug trafficking.
- **Emotional wound**: Sixteen-year-old Peggy was at a party when she heard some girls laughing about how fat she was. Peggy never went to another party.
- **Spiritual wound**: Jim never told anyone why he hated his parents' church; their spiritual leader had abused him when he was a boy.

The more real the key-characters are to the storyteller, the more the listeners will be drawn to hear the story. The storyteller must make his characters come alive by knowing detailed, factual information about each key-character. The storyteller needs to visualize the characters' physical aspects, their feelings, their history, their reactions, their motives and their relationships. The storyteller must see his characters with clarity if he expects his listeners to see them at all. The depth of the storyteller's knowledge of a character can be compared to an iceberg: listeners only hear about ten percent of what the storyteller knows about each character. The storyteller's knowledge of his characters deepens the story, even if most of the information never appears directly in the story.

The storyteller must paint a picture of the key-character(s) with the spoken word. He needs to develop the art of using one sentence to describe a person so completely that his listeners will have a picture of the character in their mind.

Build a character through action and dialogues, not through description. Dialogue can include internal dialogue, where a character talks to himself. Also, describe the character's emotions through action.

Give details to make each character specific and unique. Small details are helpful for making a story-character come alive. For example, saying that a farmer's hair stuck up like a rooster tail makes him different from other farmers.

Use nouns and verbs to make a character come alive. An adjective or an adverb probably means the storyteller used an inadequate verb or noun to start with. Don't say someone walks slowly when you can say he pokes, shambles, lumbers, strolls, lolls or saunters.

Show, don't tell. Don't use abstract descriptions to describe a character; use concrete descriptions. Don't describe a character by saying, "She was so beautiful." Instead, give details that will lead your listeners to conclude, "She was beautiful." For example, you could say, "When she walked down the street, truck drivers slowed down to stare at her. Young men who passed her on the street turned their heads and gazed at her."

Make a character come alive by giving him both character-consistence and finding paradoxes within his character. Characters should be consistent. Credible characters have a kind of core personality that defines who they are and gives the listeners expectations about how they will act. A consistent character has qualities that imply other qualities. An adult who grew up on the farm would be expected to know about animal care, gardening, repairing tractors and cars, and be able to read weather patterns. A lover of classical music would be expected to appreciate fine art.

Adding paradoxes to consistencies creates fascinating and unique characters. Paradoxes do not destroy the consistencies; they add to the character and prevent him from being predictable or stereotype. Paradoxes enable a character to do the unpredictable and they surprise the listeners. I know a Baptist pastor who is consistently conservative in his theology, his clothes, his hair cut, his pick-up truck, the books he reads, the music he enjoys, the jokes he tells, and his politics. But a certain paradox makes him unique and fascinating. After a heart attack that resulted in bypass surgery, he bought a Harley Davidson motorcycle. On his day off, he takes day long outings with other bikers. His congregation discovered that he has always read motorcycle magazines and is as knowledgeable about motorcycles as he is about the Bible.

Give characters pronounceable names. Do not give different characters similar names unless they are twins.

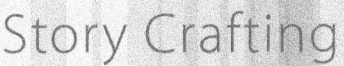

KEY-CHARACTER INFORMATION FORM

This form can help you develop information about your key-characters. Remember, story-listeners only hear about ten percent of what you, the storyteller, know about each character. Your detailed knowledge of your key-characters deepens the story, even if you never mention most of the information in the story. Prepare one of these forms for each key-character. Fill out as may descriptions as possible.

Name of Character _____

Sex _____ Age _____ Birth Date _____

Height _____ Weight _____ Build _____ Physical Condition _____

Race _____ Ethic Orientation _____ Nationality _____

Social Status _____

Occupation _____ Weekly Work Hours _____

Non-working Activities _____

Financial Condition _____

Marital Status _____ People in Family _____

Education _____ Hobbies _____

Religion _____

Basic Beliefs _____

_____

Disabilities or Defects _____

Abnormalities _____

Hair Color _____ Hair Length _____ Hair Style _____

General Appearance (handsome, sexy, fat, trim, meticulous, tidy, rumpled, etc.) _____

Appearance (virile, effeminate, manly, feminine, etc.) _____

Distinguishing Physical Characteristic _____

Crafting a Story

Physical Idiosyncrasies (pulling earlobe, rubbing nose, scratching head, biting nails, hands in pocket, arms crossed, popping knuckles, rattling coins in pocket, twisting buttons on clothes, etc.)

_____

Dress Custom (flashy, stylish, casual, sloppy, etc.) _____

Normal Standing Posture (weight on one foot, feet apart, slouched, erect, etc.) _____

Normal Sitting Posture (legs apart, legs crossed, feet crossed, slouched, erect, etc.) _____

Speech Accent _____ Dialect _____

Distinguishing Vocal Characteristics _____

Speech Characteristic (flattering, blunt, sharp, rude, polished, etc.) _____

Speech Idiosyncrasies (constantly clearing throat, speaking from side of mouth, etc.) _____

_____

Speech Addictions (murmuring "un-hum," repeating a word, etc.) _____

Catch Phrases (expressions that keep reappearing in speech) _____

_____

Addictions (tobacco, alcohol, drugs, pervese behavior) _____

When does he indulge in his addiction _____

Effect of addiction _____

Basic Character Description (honest, manipulative, etc.) _____

Personality Description (extrovert, introvert, hesitant, confident, cat-like, etc.) _____

_____

Abilities _____

Weaknesses _____

Consistent Characteristics _____

Paradoxes Found in Character _____

Character's Story-goal (primary ambition, dream or desire of great importance) _____

_____

Write a brief paragraph that gives a concise description of character:

Story Crafting

2. Set-up the initial-situation of the story

The initial-situation establishes the setting of the story. It answers the questions:

- What is the historical setting for the story?
- When and where did the story take place?
- Who are the key-characters in the story?

The initial-situation puts the listeners into a situation that has a history and presents the back-story, the essential details about the key-characters' past that story-listeners need to know. The initial-situation introduces the key-character who lives in a clearly described time and place. The key-character comes to the story with certain attitudes, actions, and emotions.

Use your five senses in establishing the initial-situation. Make use of smells, sights, sounds, tastes, and touching sensations. Sensual details help the story come alive and be believable.

Establish the initial-situation by saying everything that needs to be said in as few words as possible.

2.1 Develop the art of caricature to introduce the character(s)

Develop the art of caricature to introduce characters. An artist uses caricature to capture a personality, using a minimum number of brush strokes. In storytelling, caricature portrays a person with the smallest number of words. Develop the art of using one sentence to describe a person so completely that your listeners will picture him in their minds when the sentence is finished.

2.2 Spell out the story-goal of the key-character(s)

The initial-situation should introduce the story-goal of the key-character(s). The key-character's story-goals present the ambition, need, dream or object of desire that is of great importance to him.

The storyteller must determine the story-goal that is

Crafting a Story

motivating his character(s). If motive is missing, characters can go through all sorts of delightful, tragic, or hair-raising adventures and the story won't be worth listening to.

A group of co-workers went to lunch. Joe tells a story about his daughter and son-in-law coming with the grandchildren to the tenth anniversary of his daughter's high school graduation. Joe sent his wife to a church meeting and he stayed home and put the grandchildren to bed. His reason for staying home is he wanted to watch the basketball play-offs on TV. He put the grandchildren to bed before it was time for the play-offs. His grandson asked him to sit on his bed and tell him a bedside story. Then the granddaughter wanted him to sit on her bed and tell her a story. The grandson was afraid of the dark. The granddaughter didn't want the hall lights on; she wanted a night light in their room. The grandson wanted water to drink, and then the granddaughter. The grandson had to go to the bathroom, then the granddaughter. Joe held everyone's attention as he described how the manipulating nose-pickers kept him from watching the basketball game.

Then someone asked George, "How did you break your arm?"

George answered, "Car wreck."

The co-worker asked, "When did it happen?"

George answered, "Last night."

The co-worker asked, "How did it happen?"

George said, "Bank robbers were fleeing from the police and ran me off the road."

Then the co-worker turns back to Joe and asks, "Tell us more about the grandchildren's visit."

Joe gave himself a story-goal: Watch the play-offs on TV. He turned an ordinary event into a fascinating story with his grandchildren's progressive manipulations to keep him away from the TV. George had experienced a hair-raising adventure, but without a story-goal, he couldn't hold anyone's attention.

Story Crafting

Usually, it is the story-goal of the key-character(s) that will drive him to face the initial-problem. This keeps the story from ending when the initial-problem appears. Stories are about characters who want something and don't know how to get it, or they are prevented by internal or external forces from getting what they want.

The character's story-goal could be something concrete:
- More money
- A prized antique
- A job
- A companion
- An inheritance
- A new car

The story-goal could be an abstract goal such as:
- The respect of an employer
- Reciprocated love
- The appreciation of a parent
- The expiation of guilt
- A second chance
- Hope that another person would change their mind
- Hope that another person would stop unacceptable behavior
- Hope that circumstances would change
- Emotional survival
- Freedom from groundless fear

The story-goal could be a combination of the abstract and the tangible. For example: The accountant who feels worthless sitting behind a desk could see the acquisition of a cabin on the lake as the key to regaining his self-respect.

2.3 Establish the key-time

Listeners need to know at the beginning of the story the period of time when the story took place. Give descriptive details that will help them remember the time when the story begins and the time-line as the story continues. Is the story set in the past, in history? Is it set in the present, in the contemporary world? Is it set in the future, at a hypothetical time? Is it set in a fantasy time in which time is unknown and irrelevant?

2.4 Establish the key-location

Listeners need to know where the events occurred. Make them aware of the story's specific geography. Create a sketch with words and the listeners will fill in the sketch with their imaginations to make a full-blown picture.

Develop the art of using words to sketch out for the listener's imagination a description of the location. Develop the skill of giving vivid descriptions with few details and few words. Use concrete words that enable the listeners to experience the location with all his senses: sight, sound, smell, taste, touch, plus emotions.

The listeners will get restless if the storyteller takes a long time to describe the key-location. The storyteller needs to describe a few key details and then describe other details as needed while the action of the story is taking place.

3. Describe the initial-problem

A common characteristic found in stories is that the initial-situation presented the story-goal of the key-character or characters. Then, an initial-problem appears in the form of a person or circumstance which threatens to deny the key-character(s) his story-goal. The initial-problem is an inciting event that throws life out of balance for the key-character, sets the story into action, and creates a turning point. It creates a threat, a setback, a sense of menace or tension and propels the key-character in an active pursuit of his story-goal.

The initial-problem becomes the "big hook" that incites and captures the listeners' attention. It creates a hunger for the knowledge of how the key-character will obtain his story-goal.

The initial-problem presents the **external problem**(s) or **internal flaw**(s) a character faces, and the risks and dangers associated

Story Crafting

with it. There must be some danger the key-character must face, such as physical or emotional danger, or damage to one's reputation, career, relationships or self-image.

An **external-problem** comes from outside the character. It comes from an opponent or adversary. The external-problem may be:

- Another character
- An animal
- A divine being
- A force of nature
- A situation beyond the character's control
- Conflict with family, friends, loved ones

An **internal-problem** comes from a flaw within the person. The internal-problem may be:

- A character flaw
- Lack of wisdom
- A doubt
- A fear
- Confusion
- Something he is doing wrong

It is the risk and danger associated with the initial-problem that attracts listeners to a story. The story-goal of the key-character(s) must give him a vested interest in overcoming the initial-problem. He must have something at risk that will drive him to struggle.

Examples of initial-problems found in stories are many:

- An enemy
- A conflict
- An oppression
- A discrimination
- A contradiction

- A danger (real or imagined)
- An unreachable goal
- Incorrect information
- An unmet need
- An unfilled desire
- A character flaw
- More than one person seeking a goal that can be obtained by only one
- An outside interference
- A temptation to do something wrong
- An opportunity that is contrary to the key-character's ethical or moral standards
- A barrier to achieve the key-character's desires

The initial-problem gives the story-listeners a sense that something is imminent, that certain events are set in relentless motions and that bigger problems are on the way. It helps the listeners see trouble is coming before the key-crisis actually arrives.

4. Identify the key-crisis

The key-crisis is the climax of the story. It is the most exciting and suspenseful event and is built up from preceding conflicts. The first conflict begins with the initial-problem, then follows a progression of conflicts, setbacks, and dilemmas until the key-character confronts face-to-face the most powerful dilemma in the story. The key-crisis forces the key-character to make a choice or take an action in a last effort to achieve his story-goal.

The key-crisis removes the key-character from his comfort zone and requires the character to make adjustments to a new world as a part of living with a critical change.

A crisis may be a disturbance outside the character's control, or it may be a positive change or chosen alteration. Therefore, both

Story Crafting

getting fired from a job and choosing to accept a new job can put a person in a crisis situation. Hearing the doctor say, "It is cancer," brings on a crisis outside the character's control. Also, hearing the doctor tell a newly married couple, "You are pregnant!" brings on a crisis of adjusting to a new positive situation. Deciding to quit smoking and to start jogging in order to have better health brings on a crisis because of chosen positive changes.

The initial-problem is not the key-crisis. The character's struggles to resolve the initial-problems result in a series of actions, setbacks, dilemmas, progressive confrontations, and conflicts until the key-crisis is faced.

Examples of undesirable crisis events:
- Being involved in a wreck
- Becoming sick
- Failing a grade, class, test or task
- Losing a game in sports
- Losing a family member, close friend, co-worker or loved one through death
- Being fired from a job
- Losing invested money
- Experiencing a fire destroying important possessions
- Losing a pet that runs away or dies
- Breaking up a relationship with someone you love
- Divorcing your mate
- Being falsely accused
- Having a divorced child return home with children

Examples of positive crisis events:
- Making a decision to make changes for the better
- Committing to become free from an addiction (alcohol, drugs, tobacco, etc.)

- Deciding to give closure to a bad relationship
- Committing to a new relationship
- Going on a diet and beginning an exercise program
- Graduating from college
- Becoming engaged to be married
- Getting married
- Getting a new pet
- Having a baby
- Buying a new home
- Getting a job promotion
- Going on a dream vacation
- Beginning a sought-after retirement
- Gaining recognition and honor

The storyteller should think though the widest range of possible crisis events in order to expand the possibility for discovering stories.

5. Organize the sequence of events

Remember, the initial-situation gives the setting for the story and the key-character's story-goal. The initial-problem shakes up the initial-situation and propels the key-character on a quest to reach his story-goal. Then follows a series of events as the story develops with its pattern of problems, dilemmas, conflicts, setbacks, and aborted attempts at reaching the story-goal until the story has a final result. Each event that complicates the problem, or each attempt at finding a resolution, is an event within the story. Each subdivision, plot, plan, turn of events or new development is an event within the story.

The sequence of events include a progression of complicated events that make life difficult for the story-characters. They face more and more conflict situations as one obstacle after another hinders them in reaching their story-goal.

Story Crafting

The sequence of events would be the story plan written in simple outline form. It is the road map that gives direction to the story. It should first be written using one-or-two sentence statements to describe each event in the order that it will be told. This is a tool for the storyteller and may be too cryptic for anyone but the storyteller to follow. After he is satisfied with his cryptic sequence of events, the storyteller may expand on each event from its one or two sentences to turn them into paragraphs.

While determining the series of events from the beginning until the end of the story, pay special attention to description, dialogue, conflict, contrast and outside intervention.

5.1 Within the sequence of events, use concrete description

While telling the episodes in the story, use concrete description. Most of your listeners have five senses. A good storyteller enables them to mentally see, smell, hear, taste and touch each event of the story being heard.

Use specific details to give concrete descriptions. Describe background colors, the weather, sounds, tastes, and so on. Details like hair styles, brand names, gestures, habits and mannerisms give stories the voice of authority. Details can be actions, behaviors, use of language, gestures, the clothes one wears, speech mannerisms, the way a person laughs, or the unique approaches a person takes to a situation.

The storyteller should describe people and places, even if his listeners already know those people and places. The storyteller's perspective is unique; therefore, even in a familiar story, he should give detailed, concrete descriptions. Detailed descriptions of scenes and actions make a story come alive.

The storyteller should show, not tell. Instead of using abstract descriptive words, he should use concrete descriptive words.

Avoid Abstract Descriptive Words	Use Concrete Descriptive Words
She was a lousy housekeeper.	Spider webs were scattered throughout the house. Yesterday's unwashed dishes were still in the sink.
He was angry at his opponent.	He raised his voice as he shook his finger in his opponent's face.
She was beautiful.	Young men, who passed her on the street, turned their heads to gazed at her.
He was a wild teenager.	His friends called him Mad-dog. He knew all the local cops by name. Most had given him a ride in the backseat of their patrol cars.

5.2 Within the sequence of events, use dialogue for emphasis

The storyteller must have – or at least develop – an ear for the way people talk. Dialogue must appear natural, smooth and spontaneous. Find a good spot to listen to people as they interact and talk around you. This will help you create authentic dialogue. Pay attention to how people converse, the words they use and how they play off each other throughout a conversation. Incorporate real people's dialogue into your storytelling.

Dialogue must sound like talk. It should contain the same errors people make in daily conversations. It should contain a rapid exchange of short speeches. Break ideas into a series of short, simple constructed, informally spoken sentences. Dialogue should sound like people talking. It should contain grammatical mistakes that people normally make in their conversations. Use informal and natural vocabulary, complete with contractions and slang. Dialogue doesn't require complete sentences. Notice the words not voiced; observe what is said

Story Crafting

with body language and gestures.

Storytelling dialogue must have the spontaneity of real-life speech; however, it is nothing like real-life speech. Real-life speech is often interrupted, abbreviated, distracted, filled with irrelevancies and departures from the main subject. It often seems to have no direction. People ramble on and on, forget their point and use an array of sounds and comments that would be distracting to story-listeners.

Storytelling dialogue is crafted to be a carefully timed give-and-take. It should seldom contain sounds like "uh" and "um." The storyteller's dialogue should reflect real conversations; however, he shouldn't bore his listeners with the pleasantries of mundane conversation. He should get right to the point. Dialogue requires compression and economy. It must say the maximum in the fewest possible words.

Each dialogue exchange must be working towards an end to justify its use. Use dialogue for emphasis. Use dialogue for revealing a person's thoughts, flaws and character. Use dialogue for revealing each character's distinct personality and voice. Use dialogue for cultivating a character's individual style and mannerisms. Use dialogue to bring relationships into sharp focus. Also, use dialogue for showing the contrast or similarities of two characters.

Use dialogue to build personality and place. Notice how the speech of two waitresses from two different eating establishments reveals both personalities and location.

1st <u>Waitress:</u>   "Hello, my name is Jill and I will be serving you tonight. May I take your order now or would you like more time?"

2nd <u>Waitress:</u>   "Sweetie, what you gonna have tonight?"

Which of the two waitress is a college student working part time and which is the wife of the local mechanic? Which establishment has cloth napkins, and which has a roll of paper towels standing on the table? Which establishment has perfumed soap in the bathroom, and which has a dispenser for removing grease beside the soap dispenser?

Dialogue can include interior dialogue, where the character talks to himself or where he thinks out loud.

The storyteller should have only two people at a time carrying on a dialogue. A police film may have two police officers, the suspect and his lawyer in a room and all four dialogue. However, in oral storytelling, only two people at a time should carry on a dialogue.

When using dialogue, first, identify the speaker, then quote his dialogue. Avoid identifying the speaker during the middle or at the end of the quotation.

<u>Do</u>: *John said,* "I'm hungry for fish. Let's do Catfish House."

<u>Do not</u>: "I'm hungry for fish," *John said,* "Let's do Catfish House."

<u>Do not</u>: "I'm hungry for fish; let's do Catfish House," *said John*.

The storyteller doesn't need to tell what a line of dialogue means or what its emotional impact is.

<u>Don't say</u>: Sally exclaimed *vehemently,* "I'm fed up with you and your excuses!"

<u>Do say</u>: Sally exclaimed, "I'm fed up with you and your excuses!"

If the listener can't catch the exclamation or the vehemence from hearing the dialogue, the storyteller didn't do his job.

5.3 Within the sequence of events, conflict adds spice to a story

Conflict and crisis add spice to a story. Conflict is the soul of a story. The greater the conflict, the greater the attention of the listeners. The key-character has his story-goal which is a personal desire or life objective. He must struggle against forces that block that desire. He must crash into cruel, uncooperative situations or people, and deal with opposing forces. A story worth listening to doesn't just portray the rosy side. It portrays the dark side of life and deals with antagonistic events. Conflict may be real or imaginary.

Dilemma creates conflict. A dilemma either involves the

necessity of making the choice of two or more good things or the lesser of two or more evils. A dilemma is created when the key-character must choose between two positives or two negatives.

A dilemma between irreconcilable positives would have two options; both are really good but only one can be attained. The key-character desires two things, but circumstances force him to choose only one. A young man enjoys eating daily with two female co-workers who are roommates and best friends. Sara is good looking, well organized, reserved, and conservative in her spending. He would like to take Sara out to lunch and then go on a long walk through the park. Jane is a knockout beauty, extravagant, spontaneous, and the life of any party, but the young man could never afford Jane's expensive taste for clothing and jewelry. He would love to invite Jane to go to some parties. The young man needs a date for a Valentine Banquet. He knows that if he were to ask one of them out, the other would never betray her best friend and go out with him. Sara would make a better wife, Jane would be more fun at a party. He wants to date them both and has a dilemma as to which one to ask out.

A dilemma between negatives would require the key-character to decide which is the lesser of evils, and neither choice would give him what he wants. Both choices are undesirable. He wants neither, but circumstances force him to choose one. A young man is excited about getting married after graduating from a university with a Ph.D. in philosophy. He is elated about a job offer to teach philosophy in a small university. However, a downturn in the economy forces the university to withdraw its job offer. The young man is faced with a dilemma, delay his wedding until he finds a teaching job, or go to work with his future father-in-law in the family-owned plumbing and septic tank construction firm.

Conflict requires adaptation. It creates a turning point that changes the condition of a character's life. It removes the key-character from his comfort zone and requires him to adjust. Conflict attracts the listeners' attention as a magnet attracts metal.

Some situations that provide conflict:
- A serious disagreement or argument
- An unmet need
- A dilemma
- A betrayal
- Two people with the same goal, but only one can obtain it
- A barrier that prevents a person from reaching his goals
- A struggle against an opponent
- An incompatibility between opinions, principles, etc.
- A conflict of interest in which the characters is in a situation that is incompatible or at variance with his ethical moral standard, situation, or position

After establishing the initial-problem, organize the sequence of events until the story reaches a crisis. Describe how the main character enters and goes through all the throes of the critical event. Show how he lives through the crisis, how he gets help, how he makes right or wrong decisions.

5.4 Within the sequence of events, moral-character is revealed by choices made under pressure

The storyteller needs to be aware of the distinction between characterizing and revealing moral-character. To characterize is to give observable qualities of a story-character. It gives information that could be discovered by observing him and taking notes about him day in and day out. To reveal moral-character is to show the moral or ethical qualities that distinguish the story-character.

To characterize is to give such information as:
- Forty-year-old construction worker
- Married with two children and another on the way
- Six feet six inches tall and muscle-bound. Neighborhood children consider him a gentle giant
- Unemployed due to slow-down in constructions

Story Crafting

- Has the speech idiosyncrasies of always clearing throat before speaking

To reveal moral-character is to show moral or ethical qualities that distinguishes the story-character. Moral-character describes the moral or ethical strengths or weaknesses of the story-character. Examples are:

- Honest or deceitful
- Kind or cruel
- Generous or stingy
- Courageous or cowardly

Moral-character is revealed by the decisions the story-character makes when he is under stress. Great stress is needed to reveal moral-character.

The following is an example of putting a story-character under stress to reveal his moral-character:

It had been two months since John received his last unemployment check as a construction worker. His wife is due with their third child, and they lost medical insurance coverage when he was laid off. Complications with the pregnancy resulted in unexpected medical bills, and as a result John missed two payments on their house and three on his Ford F-150 pick-up truck. John explained his situation to the vice-president of the bank. The vice-president told him, "If you don't make payments next month, we will began procedures to foreclose on your house and repossess your truck."

John walked out of the bank and saw a billfold lying on the sidewalk. He picked it up, intending to return it to its owner. He opened the billfold, found the name and address of its owner, and he saw a thick stack of one-hundred dollar bills.

John's choice when he is under great financial stress and finds lots of money inside a lost billfold will reveal his moral-character. Whatever choice John makes will give the story-listeners a grasp of his moral-character.

Show, don't tell. Don't say your story-character is honest, or dependable, or selfish, or cruel. Put him in a stressful situation

49

where the choices made reveal his moral and ethical strength or weakness.

5.5 Determine where the key-crisis happens in the sequence of events

The key-crisis is the climax of the story and is usually built up from preceding conflicts. Determine where the key-crisis happens in the sequence of events.

6. Establish the final-situation of the story

The story continues until a conclusion is reached that establishes a final-situation. In the process of living through complications of crises, the key-character either gets help, gains new insights, makes new choices, gains skills to face future crises, has a change of character; or refuses to change and continues with the same flaws or inappropriate actions. If the crisis experience brought new learning, new insight, new ability, or change of character; the main character will never be the same. The final-situation may be an affirmation with the character meeting a similar crisis in a way that affirms that he is different from when he met the initial-problem.

The initial-problem that disturbed the initial-situation usually has a connection to the final-situation that follows the main character going through a crisis.

The final-situation answers questions such as the following:

- How did the story end?
- How was the initial-problem solved or the story-goal met after the key-character faced a crisis?
- What were the results of improper action taken in an attempt to resolve the key-crisis?
- What is the connection between the initial-problem that disturbed the initial-situation and the final-situation that established the outcome?

Story Crafting

REVISING THE CRAFTED STORY

After the storyteller has crafted the structure of his story, he needs to make revisions. He needs to give special attention to key-repetitions and key-attitudes. He needs to transform "telling" into "showing," and he needs to reduce the story to the essential facts.

1. **Work on key-repetitions**

Events in an oral story are often tied together by words, themes, patterns, facts or ideas that are repeated, either exactly or with minor variations. The storyteller should intentionally use repetition in order to emphasize, to build a climax or to express strong emotions. Repetition helps the listeners recall the key elements of the story. Therefore, the storyteller should determine what needs to be repeated.

Repetitions in a story can take a variety of forms. Certain words, the same phrase, the same theme, similar actions, a song, a chant, the same gesture, certain patterns, facts or ideas can be repeated; either exactly or with minor variations. Repetitions help both the storyteller and listeners to remember.

In the story of "The Three Little Pigs," each of the three little pigs built a house (action). The wolf knocked on each little pig's door (action) and said, "Little pig, little pig, let me come in" (words). Each of the three little pigs answered, "No, no, not by the hair of my chinny chin chin; I will not let you come in" (words). Each time, the wolf answered, "Then I'll huff and I'll puff and I'll blow your house in" (words). Twice the wolf huffed and puffed and blew the house in (action).

Notice how repeated crisis cycles often appear in life stories.

Families may choose favorite crises and go through them over and over. For example, they may take yearly, dull vacations. Another example is the person who is always going on a new diet. People often repeat the same behavior over and over. They would rather repeat familiar habits than learn to deal with uncertain changes.

In some stories, patterns are repeated, ranging from addictive behavior to repetitive moving, constant job changes and ongoing schooling. In other stories, the same words or chants are repeatedly woven into the story. In others, similar themes are repeated.

Review the sequence-of-events to determine if repetitions have already been included or if more need to be inserted. Most storytellers need to weave repetitions into their story after establishing the sequence of events.

2. Consider key-attitudes to be expressed in the story

Stories express attitudes, feelings, values, and emotions. The storyteller needs to determine the attitudes he wishes to express in the story in order to help his listeners feel the desired emotions.

Characters have attitudes toward themselves, other characters, certain values, events and certain issues. A character's attitudes express the opinions, the point of view, and the slant that a character takes toward other characters and toward certain events.

Characters express attitudes. A beginning list of the categories of characters' basic attitudes could be described as: mad, sad, glad and scared. Each category implies other attitudes.

- ■ *Mad* implies: anger, rage, frustration, hostility, irateness, resentment...
- ■ *Sad* implies: sorrowful, woeful, depressed, hopeless, discouraged...
- ■ *Glad* implies: pleased, happy, content, cheerful, joyful, ecstatic...
- ■ *Scared* implies: fear, terror, horror, panic, anguish, anxiety...

Story Crafting

Within the story, use actions to present the character's attitudes. Show, don't tell. Instead of saying the mother was concerned about her son, describe the mother sitting up until the son returned home. Instead of saying the key-character was angry, describe his actions. For example: "His arms were folded across his chest and his hands were clenched into a fist."

Add descriptions that stimulate the listeners' five senses and help them see, hear, taste, smell, and feel everything going on. Use descriptions to get people to experience emotions as you tell the story.

Review the story's sequence-of-events and consider what attitude the storyteller desires to express with each event and with each character. Then make revisions or additions that include concrete descriptions, actions and dialogues which convey those attitudes. Avoid telling a fact if you can show emotion to the fact with dialogue, action or description.

3. **Transform "telling" into "showing"**

Show, don't tell. Review your story to find where you told instead of showed. The storyteller should not put listeners on his knees like they were little children and explain the story to them. Give them concrete facts and let them reach their own conclusions.

If you used abstract descriptions to describe a character or setting, transform it into concrete descriptions. If you said something similar to, "George was a poor dirty child," transform it to, something like, "Little ten-year-old George looked at his torn, ragged, unwashed, unpatched overalls. His mother had not told him to take a bath, so he had not taken a bath before going to church. He looked down at his dirty bare feet."

If you told about your story-character's moral-character, revise your story by putting him in a stressful situation where the choices made reveal his moral and ethical strength or weakness. Instead of saying, "Andrew was cruel," say, "After fighting with his girlfriend, Andrew ran off the side of the road in order to run over a dog."

If you described an attitude, revise your story to show the attitude. Don't say, "Martha was sad," when you can say, "Martha woke up with her pillow wet from tears."

4. Reduce the story to the essential facts

When preparing the story, most storytellers include needless details that clutter the story and take unnecessary time to tell. Remember the principle: "Less is more," when revising the story. The less there is in the story, the more impact it has. Therefore, anything that can be cut should be cut. If narration can be removed and the story could still stand on its feet, then cut it. Eliminate all needless details and get the story down to the essential facts. Eliminate all dialogue, facts and events that aren't essential to move the story forward. The storyteller will probably need to eliminate 20% to 50% of the material he included in the first crafting of his story.

This is hard for me to do. When I finish crafting a new story, I feel like I've given birth to a baby. It is hard to do surgery, cutting off and throwing away parts of my baby. Yet, I have learned that such surgery and throwing away is needed to improve my story. Drastic surgery is needed to get my crafted stories ready to tell. I usually take more time revising a story than I did in first crafting it.

Story Crafting

	STRUCTURE OF A STORY
BEGINNING	**INITIAL-SITUATION** It gives background information on the: - **Key-character** - **Key-time** - **Key-location** of the story - Key-character's **story-goal**
	INITIAL- PROBLEM It presents the episode that disturbs the **initial-situation** and indicates that trouble is on the way.
MIDDLE	**SEQUENCE OF EVENTS** The story develops with a series of events that include pattern of problems, conflicts, outside intervention and aborted attempts at resolution. The **sequence of events** pays attention to description, dialogue, conflict, contrast and outside intervention. Within the sequence of events, the **key-crisis** happens.
ENDING	**FINAL-SITUATION** The story ends with the final result. The conclusion establishes the **final-situation**.
	Key-attitudes are expressed and **key-repetitions** occur throughout the story.

Story Crafting

REORGANIZING YOUR CRAFTED STORY FOR TELLING

After crafting your story, reorganize it, using the following structure.

KEY-ELEMENTS OF THE STORY

    Key-character(s):

        Characters mentioned in the initial-situation:

        Other characters mentioned during the telling of the story:

    Story-goal of the key-character(s):

    Key-time:

    Key-location:

    Key-crisis:

    Key-repetitions:

    Key-attitudes:

STRUCTURE OF THE STORY

    Initial-situation:

    Initial-problem:

    Sequence of events:

    Final-situation:

Story Crafting

EXAMPLE OF REORGANIZING A CRAFTED STORY FOR TELLING:

DRAWING OF THE BEAST

Jackson Day adapted an old folk tale to craft this story.

Analysis of the Story

KEY-ELEMENTS OF THE STORY

Key-characters: The king and the wood carver

>**Characters mentioned in the initial-situation:** king, king's wise men

>**Other characters mentioned during the telling of the story:** artist, soldiers

Key-characters' story-goal:

>The king was determined to have his dream interpreted.

>The wood carver was determined to do an accurate drawing of the beast of the king's dream.

Key-time: Ancient history, during a fantasy time in which time is unknown and irrelevant

Key-location: The king's palace

Key-crisis: The wood carver appeared before the king without his drawing of the beast of the king's dream

Key-repetitions:

- Description of the beast of the king's dream

- The king's promise of rewards to the artist who could draw the beast, or punishment if he failed

- The wise men and the artists greeted the king, "May the king live forever. Your highness..."

- The wood carver greeted the king, "Your highness..."

- The word, "dream"

- The word, "details"
- The wood carver's attention to details
- The soldiers' inability to find the wood carver

Key-attitudes:
- The king's desire to have his dream interpreted
- The reverence, the wise men, and the artists showed for the king
- The king's frustration when artists failed to draw the beast of his dream
- The artists' greed for wealth and honor
- The wood carver's confidence in his ability to draw the beast
- The wood carver's quest for details

STRUCTURE OF THE STORY

Initial-situation of the story

There was a mighty king of a vast empire. The king's wise men counseled him and interpreted his dreams. The king believed that the gods spoke to him through his dreams. Since the king could not understand his dreams, he needed wise men to interpret them.

Initial-problem

The king had a reoccurring dream about a beast.

Sequence of events

- A king had wise men to counsel him and interpret his dreams.
- The king had a reoccurring dream about a beast.
- The king's wise men skipped details of the dream in their interpretations. They said that if they could see the beast, they could interpret the king's dream.
- The king promised the artists rewards if they drew the beast of his dream, or punishment if they failed.
- Renowned artists failed and were sentenced to death.
- A wood carver said he could draw the beast of the king's dream.

- The wood carver promised to draw the beast if the king described it so the wood carver could see it in his mind.

- The king described his dream and the wood carver asked for more details.

- After a week of questioning the king, the wood carver said he could see the beast in his mind and would return in six months with the drawing.

- The wood carver fled to the great woods where the soldiers could not find him.

- Six months to the day, an hour before sunset, the wood carver returned to the king without the drawing.

- The wood carver prepared charcoal pencils and drew the beast, taking fifteen minutes.

- The king asked the wood carver why he kept him waiting for six months.

- The wood carver said he needed six months to gain the ability to draw the beast in fifteen minutes.

Final-situation of the story

The wood carver said he needed six months to gain the ability to draw the beast in fifteen minutes.

THE STORY

A long, long, time ago, there was a mighty king of a vast empire. The king's wise men counseled him and interpreted his dreams. The king and his wise men were convinced that the gods spoke to him through his dreams. The king could not understand his dreams, so he needed wise men to interpret them.

The king had a reoccurring dream about a beast with the body of a bull, a tail like a snake, and hooves like a horse. From the shoulders of the bull appeared the body of a man who had the face of a lion with antlers on his head, like those of a deer.

The king dreamed about the beast two or three times each week.

His wise men could not interpret the dream to the king's satisfaction. They always skipped some details of the dream in their interpretations. The wise men told the frustrated king, "May the king live forever. Your highness, if we could only see the beast in your dream, we could interpret your dream."

The king called in renowned artists. He told them, "I will give honor and wealth to the artist who draws the beast of my dream; however, I will sentence to death the artist whose drawing does not look like the beast of my dream."

The king's words filled the artists with dreams of wealth and honor. Each artist told the king, "May the king live forever. Your highness, describe the beast in your dream, and I will draw it for you."

The king described the beast, "It has the body of a bull, a tail like a snake, hooves like a horse, the trunk of a man, and a face like a lion with antlers, like a deer."

The renowned artists rushed to draw the beast. Each wanted to be the first to finish his drawing and to receive wealth and honor from the king. However, when each artist displayed his drawing, details were missing and the king said, "That is not the drawing of the beast that I see in my dream." Each artist was sentenced to death.

There was a wood carver who made carvings of animals. Before each carving, he would use charcoal from his fireplace and do a detailed drawing of the animal. Then he would carve his drawing from a piece of wood. On market day he would sell his carvings.

One market day, one of the king's wise men was admiring the details in the carving of a horse. The wood carver told the wise man, "If the king were to describe the details of the beast of his dream so that I could see it in my mind, I could draw it for him."

The wise man took the wood carver to the king. The king said, "Renowned artists have not been able to draw the beast of my dream. They were sentenced to death. Do you think you can draw the beast of my dream?"

Story Crafting

The wood carver replied, "If your highness, the king, will describe the details of the beast of his dream, so that I can see him in my mind, I will draw it for him."

The king replied, "I will give honor and wealth to you if you draw the beast of my dream; however, I will give you the death sentence if your drawing does not look like the beast in my dream." Then the king described the beast of his dream, "It has the body of a bull, a tail like a snake, hooves like a horse, the trunk of a man, a face like a lion, and antlers like a deer."

The wood carver asked for more details, "The tail that is like a snake, is the head of the snake at the end of the tail or is it attached to the beast? What kind of snake is it? How long is the snake? How thick is the snake? The markings on the snake, are they clear and defined like those of a snake that just exited the river, or are they dull like a snake that has been crawling on a dusty road?" After hours of questioning the king, the wood carver said, "Now I can see in my mind the tail that looks like a snake. Tomorrow I will return for more details." After returning to the king's palace every day for a week, the wood carver told the king, "Your highness, now I see the beast of the king's dream in my head. In six months, I shall return and show your highness and your wise men the drawing of the beast of the king's dream."

The king replied, "Other artists only needed hours. The one who took the longest needed a week. You want six months?"

The wood carver replied, "Your highness, those artists did not draw the beast of your dreams to your satisfaction. They were sentenced to death. I will return in six months."

The king declared, "You have six months from sundown today to show me the beast of my dream or you will be sentenced to death."

The wood carver left the king's presence. A week later, the king sent soldiers to determine the progress that the wood carver was making on his drawing. But the wood carver had left home to live in the great woods. His family did not know where he was. The king thought the man had lied about his skills and had fled to hide in the great woods. The king sent the soldiers to the great woods. But they could not find the wood carver.

As time passed, the soldiers intensified their search in the great woods, but they could not find the wood carver.

On the morning when the six months deadline was up, the wood carver did not appear. Neither did he appear at noon. But an hour before sundown, the wood carver appeared at the gates of the king's palace. Soldiers rushed him into the king's presence.

When the wood carver unrolled his canvas, the king was furious; the canvas was blank. The wood carver told the angry king, "Your highness the king gave me until the sun goes down. I still have an hour to draw the beast of your dream." Then the man opened a sack, removed a knife and pieces of charcoal. He began to carve the pieces of charcoal into pencils of different thicknesses. Fifteen minutes before the sun went down, the wood carver made his first marks on the canvas. He drew quickly as the king and his wise men observed the beast of the king's dream appearing on the canvas.

As the sun went down, the drawing was completed. The king exclaimed, "That is the drawing of the beast of my dream. But if you could have drawn the beast in fifteen minutes, why did you make me wait for six months?"

The wood carver replied, "Your highness, six months ago, when I left your palace, I could see the beast of your dream in my mind. But it has taken me six months to be able to draw it in fifteen minutes."

Story Crafting

TELLING AN EXISTING STORY

Many storytellers tell existing stories instead of crafting originals. Some never craft an original story, they only tell existing stories. Most craft a few originals, but mainly tell existing stories. The storyteller has a choice: he may work at crafting his own stories or he may tell stories that he finds in books or hears on the media. Another choice is to adapt and restructure stories that he finds in books or on the media, and then craft them into his own version.

It requires time and disciplined work for a storyteller to craft an original story. Yet, each person has stories from his own life that need to be told.

Storytellers find most of their stories for telling through listening or reading. They find existing stories that beg to be retold. A story found in a book or heard by another storyteller is copyrighted. However, a story idea is not copyrighted. A storyteller can find a story through listening or reading, and then revise it, adapt it, place it in another location, create different characters, insert different events, add parts of other stories into the story, and craft the story into his own. If you read or hear a story that impresses you, it will probably be meaningful to your listeners as well.

If you revise and adapt a story, it is appropriate to say, "I found the idea for this story in _____ by _____ and I have crafted it into a new story."

If you tell existing stories that you have not recrafted, respect their copyright. Teachers and librarians working within the context of their jobs are free to use material that has a copyright without asking permission of the author.

Telling an Existing Story

If you are being paid as a storyteller and wish to use another person's original stories, you should first get his permission. If you heard or read someone's personal story, you should obtain permission before telling it.

Myths, folktales and legends are owned by the public. However, a specific version told by an individual teller or found in a book is the author's or teller's copyrighted property. If you like a folktale a storyteller has told, research the story by finding other versions, and then craft your own version of the story.

Published literary tales and poetry are copyrighted material. They may be told at informal story swaps and for educational purposes. However, if you tell a story by another teller or author in a paid professional setting, you need to request the permission of the publisher or author. It is both illegal and unethical to be paid for a story crafted by an author or teller without his written permission. Respect copyright laws.

When telling a copyrighted story, the storyteller must be true to the original version. The storyteller does not have the privilege of adapting the story, leaving out details of the story, or expanding on a copyrighted story.

Even in informal story swaps or educational settings, whenever you tell a story crafted by another teller or author, you should give credit to the source of your story.

If the storyteller combined elements from several stories, it would be ethical for him to inform his listeners of the stories that were the seed-source for his new crafted story. However, it is not necessary.

I learned the hard way. Stories found on the internet or sent in e-mails with the notation, "author unknown" may be copyrighted stories. I found a story that I liked on the internet with the notation, "author unknown." Later I found the story in a book that was copyrighted.

Story Crafting

ANALYZING AN EXISTING STORY

The storyteller who determines to tell an existing story should discover the key-elements and analyze its structure as part of his preparation. He should organize the key-elements and the structure in the same way as he would a story he crafted himself.

KEY-ELEMENTS OF THE STORY

    1.   Key-character(s)

List the characters mentioned at the beginning of the story in the initial-situation, then note the characters who are added during the telling of the story.

Determine who is(are) the key-character(s).

It would be helpful to fill out the KEY-CHARACTER INFORMATION FORM on each of the key-characters.

Develop the art of caricature, using one sentence to describe each character so completely that you will have a picture of each one in your mind.

    2.   Story-goal of the key-character(s)

Find the story-goal of the key-character(s). Observe what is of greatest importance to the main character, such as his ambition, dream, or value.

    3.   Key-time

Establish the historical setting for the story to be told. Note descriptive details that will help determine the time.

4. Key-location

The storyteller needs a clear picture in his head of the place where the story occurred.

5. Key-crisis

Stories are about characters, their struggles, and their conflicts. The key-crisis is the climax of the story – the most exciting event.

6. Key-repetitions

Repetition is woven into an oral story purposely. Words, themes, patterns, facts or ideas may be repeated, either exactly or with minor variations. Repetitions are made in order to emphasize something, to build a climax or to express strong emotions. Therefore, the storyteller should make note of what is repeated in the story.

7. Key-attitudes expressed in the story

Stories express attitudes, feelings and emotions. The storyteller needs to discover the attitudes expressed in the story in order to feel and express the desired emotions when he is telling the story. He also needs to determine the attitudes he desires to express about each character, location and event in the story.

STRUCTURE OF THE STORY

1. The initial-situation

The initial-situation establishes the background and setting of the story. Find the information about the place, time and characters in the story.

Details help the story come alive and seem believable. Therefore, observe the use of smells, sounds, tastes, and touching sensations that help establish the initial-situation.

2. The initial-problem

The initial-problem is the episode that disturbs the initial-situation. The initial-problem presents the external problem(s) or internal flaw(s) a character faces, and the risks and dangers associated with it. The story-goal of the key-character(s) must require him to face the initial-problem.

3. The sequence-of-events

The initial-situation gives the background for the story. The initial-problem shakes up the initial-situation and throws the key-character off balance. A series of events follows. Each subdivision, plot, plan, turn of events or new development is an event within the story.

While observing the series of events from the beginning until the end of the story, pay special attention to description, dialogue, conflict, contrast and outside intervention.

Observe where in the sequence of events the key-crisis happens.

4. The final-situation

The storyteller needs to have the final-situation in mind so he knows when he has finished his story.

Story Crafting

ELEMENTS USED TO COMMUNICATE THE STORY
Oral Language Dimensions

All of the ingredients that have made the storyteller who he is, and that have shaped his life come into play as he tells a story. The accumulation of life experiences, hurts, pleasures, and values enter into the storyteller's experience in the telling of each story. Who the storyteller is, impacts not only the stories he chooses to tell, but also the manner in which he tells them.

In telling a story to listeners, a storyteller uses at least eight oral language dimensions: appearance, posture, gesture, eye movement, sound, attitude, feedback from the listeners, and words.

1. **Appearance**

    The storyteller makes an impression on his audience before he opens his mouth. The listeners will make a quick judgment about the storyteller based on his clothing and appearance. For women: clothes, hairstyle, use of cosmetics and jewelry, etc. create an impression. For men: clothes, hairstyle, facial hair or lack of it, etc. create a first impression. The storyteller creates an atmosphere with his choice of clothes and appearance. One should avoid clothes that distract the audience's attention from his story. The most important words for effective apparel are "be appropriate."

    The storyteller should determine the impression he wishes to make to his audience and then choose the appearance that will help him make that impression.

Story Crafting

Women should be careful with the way they sit in front of an audience. Also, a lady should be cautious to avoid jewelry that could reflect lights or make noise when she moves around. Such jewelry would distract the listener's attention from the story.

The storyteller wants his listeners to focus on his face when he is performing. Therefore, he should use clothing that will not distract from his face. For example, tattoos on a storyteller's arms would draw listeners to focus on his arms instead of his face. He should cover the tattoos with long sleeves in order to help his listeners focus on his face.

Prior to appearing before an audience, the storyteller should always brush his hair and teeth, iron his clothes, fasten zippers and buttons, and arrange his shirt (blouse) properly. He should look in a mirror before going before his listeners. Then he should check again his zipper and buttons.

There is not so much a right or wrong way to dress or groom. However, the occasion, the location, one's listeners and the impression that the storyteller wants to make dictates what he will wear. Clothes that would be appropriate for storytelling under a shade tree on a hot summer day could be inappropriate for a church accustomed to formal services. A good suggestion is to dress similarly or slightly better than the majority of the listeners present, unless the storyteller is choosing clothing to make an impression that would help him tell his story.

It is difficult to judge one's own appearance and the impression it makes on others. Therefore, a wise storyteller will request advice from family and close friends about his image and seek suggestions on how to improve it.

Be sure to wear comfortable shoes and clothes. Some storytellers stand in one position, but many move around. I use a lot of movement and feel more comfortable with loose, comfortable clothing and good running shoes, unless dress shoes and a suit are required for a formal location.

2. Posture

Good posture increases the storyteller's ability to project his voice, breathe and move comfortably. Poor body posture sends the message that one has low self-esteem. Therefore, stand tall or sit straight!

An excellent posture position for the storyteller is to use the "ready position" of an athlete, who is poised to move in any direction. Feet should be shoulder-width apart, and knees should be flexible (not locked). By leaning slightly forward with the legs slightly flexed, the storyteller could bounce up and down on the balls of his feet or move in any direction. This position sends the message that the storyteller is bursting with energy and ready to get into action.

The storyteller may choose to mime the posture of a story-character while telling his story.

3. Gesture

When the storyteller speaks, he doesn't sit or stand like a wooden carving. The storyteller moves his hands, his eyes narrow or widen, the skin around his eyes crinkles. He turns his head, touches his chin, bites his lips, or blinks back tears. The entire body speaks when the storyteller is talking. Gestures, such as the position of the feet; the movement of the trunk, arms, hands and fingers; the position of the arms; the shaking of the head; and the look in the eyes communicate messages and attitudes.

Gesture is such a powerful means of communication that it is possible for totally deaf people to communicate by using gestures organized as sign language. I have been in countries where I did not speak the language and was able to communicate and understand many things by using and observing gestures.

Certain body expressions need to be avoided unless they are deliberately used for giving emphasis. For example, avoid speaking with hands in the pocket, or hands held together behind the back, or arms crossed. Avoid leaning on a speaker's stand, table or chair. Avoid the look of the self-conscious person with an inferiority complex, whose head is bowed looking at his feet, and whose body is curved forward. Also, avoid the arrogant look of superiority, with the nose stuck up and eyes that look above the audience.

Certain gestures make the storyteller look ridiculous when they are not being used for emphasis. Some storytellers unconsciously play with their watches or the microphone wires, pop their knuckles, rattle coins in their pocket, chew on their finger nails, pull up their shirts, twist the buttons on their coat or blouse, pass their hands through their hair or rub their heads. Some even pick their nose or scratch their rear end. Other negative actions are rocking from side to side, going back and forth on one's heels and toes, or pacing back and forth. A common adverse posture pattern is turning sideways to the audience and leaning back on one hip.

Most of the time, being natural leads to the proper gestures. One can learn to communicate with the body; however, doing what comes naturally is usually best. Gestures obey a natural process. When the storyteller thinks about what he is going to say, the mind tells the body the proper movement. It is natural for the body to begin expressing itself just before the words are spoken. Natural gestures occur just before the spoken words or at the same time as the words.

Hand gestures should be expressive but never exaggerated. They should meet the needs of the story, flow naturally, and integrate with the spoken word. Usually hand gestures need to be between the waist and shoulders. Gestures should be above the belt line in order to be visible by the audience. Also, gestures below the waist give the impression of a person being shifty, secretive or insecure. Hand gestures above the shoulders need to be reserved for rare moments of exceptional emotions. Gestures above the shoulder usually mean excitement, panic, surprise or worship. A general rule to follow is the larger the auditorium, the larger and wider the gestures; the smaller the room, the smaller and more moderate the gestures.

When storytelling, always keep the scenes at the same location. For example, once you mention a tree and point toward it, make sure that every time you look toward that tree, it remains in the same spot on stage.

Gestures change with emotional levels. The storyteller, who wishes to give the impression of calm, uses gestures that are smaller and limited. When he is expressing excitement, his gestures become larger and more physical.

Avoid faking. Falsehood doesn't work. Everybody has seen bad actors at work. While it is difficult to describe simulated gestures, everybody recognizes them when they are seen. The storyteller who fakes with his gestures risks the danger of being known as a bad actor or someone who can't be trusted.

Considering the importance that the body has in communication, I recommend that the storyteller avoid hiding behind a table or other furniture. He should move his position where he can be seen by all his listeners. Chairs, tables, speaker's stands, and desks create barriers that keep the listeners from observing all of the storyteller's gestures and body movement.

Do not stand only on one side of the stage. If possible, move around. This helps all the listeners to feel involved in the storytelling event.

4.   Eye movement

The storyteller communicates with his eyes. Therefore, he should make sure he can see everyone in his audience. People he can't see, can't see him. He may need to rearrange the seating or move around during his storytelling so everyone can observe him all the time.

When the storyteller begins, he should survey all of his listeners and then begin extended eye communication with as many individuals as possible. He must remember to look at those at the far edges of the room, those in the middle, those sitting along the side of him, and even those sitting behind him. Each listener should receive

Story Crafting

a look from the storyteller. When addressing a large group, extended eye communication (five seconds or more) to people in different places in the audience is essential. When he looks at one individual, dozens of people around that person will think he is talking just to them. The listener who observes the speaker looking in his direction will feel important. The one who never sees the storyteller looking at him will feel left out and may become disinterested in the story or even reject the storyteller.

Eye movements can demonstrate that the storyteller is imagining the events and images of his story. If he looks up and to one side as he pauses, this usually suggests that he is searching his memory or thoughts. Looking straight down as he speaks suggests submission, embarrassment or absorption in his personal thoughts or feelings. When eye movements show that the storyteller is imagining the events and images of his story, they also help his listeners do the same.

Eye movements can be used as a dramatic tool to suggest the relationship between a character and the objects or people with whom the character interacts. The storyteller should face his listeners directly when he is speaking to them. However, when he is narrating a dialogue, the direction he faces can show how a conversation passes from one character in the story to another.

Eye movements can be used as a dramatic tool to suggest the relationship between a superior character to an inferior character. If I were telling a story about a kindergarten student being sent to the principal for discipline: When the principal is speaking to the child, I would look almost straight down. When the child is speaking to the principal, I would look almost straight up. If I were telling a story about an employee speaking to his boss: When the employee is speaking, I would look slightly toward my left, but look slightly up like a 5' 6" man would look up to a 6' 4" man. When the boss is speaking to the employee, I would look slightly toward my right, but look down like a 6' 4" man looking down on a 5' 6" man. But when I am narrating the story, I would look at my story-listeners.

5. Sound and silence

Speaking too loudly or too softly irritates the audience and interferes with their getting the story. Success in transmission of a message is related to volume, rhythm and voice tone. The storyteller needs to find a volume level that is comfortable for his audience.

Vocal modulation gives spice to a story. Vocal modulation can be done by changing the volume, intensity, speed of speaking, and alternating the pitch of the voice.

Sounds that are not words can express many things. The storyteller can make a clucking sound, give a sigh, slap his legs, clap his hands, snap his fingers, boo, whistle, do suction-pops with his mouth, imitate the sound of a horse trotting, a truck roaring, or a train going down the track.

If the storyteller can't make the sounds himself, he can call a sound to his listener's attention. He can say the kitten sounded like a baby crying. The car crash sounded like the trash truck picking up metal containers. The scratching sounded like tree limbs blowing against a metal roof.

The same word can be sounded out in many different ways to express different attitudes. The pitch, speed of speech, timbre, and timing can intensify the meaning of a word or even reverse its meaning. Try sounding out the three words: "I love you" in different ways to express different emotions such as doubt, anger, sarcasm, manipulation, and love.

Silence is a powerful tool for the storyteller. The language of silence and pauses can be more powerful than spoken words. Silence creates drama. A long pause may be a storyteller's exclamation mark! In the midst of spoken words, silence becomes the exception and commands the listeners' attention. Silence gives the listeners time to think about what was just said and react to it. The storyteller also needs silence for thinking and reacting to his story as he tells it.

When he is narrating a dialogue, the storyteller may pause between each character's speech, so he can react to what the last character said and adjust to the lines of the character who is replying. Pauses serve as invisible quotation marks to help the listeners realize that one character has stopped talking and another has started.

A pause can be used at the end of a series of connecting events and before starting a new sequence of events that move the story in a different direction.

6. Attitude

The storyteller expresses his feelings toward the story he is narrating. He expresses his love for the story, or his distaste for it. The storyteller will find some stories that he dislikes telling; however, he still tells them, because the stories are important to him and he feels a need to tell them. For example, I don't like telling the story of my father's death when I was 14. I don't like telling the story of taking my pregnant wife to the hospital where she had a miscarriage and we returned home with empty arms. Yet these events marked my life and I tell them to help others face crisis experiences. Most of the time I tell stories that I delight in telling. When the storyteller's attitude toward the story is transparent, he has credibility to tell it.

The storyteller expresses his feelings toward his audience; such as, whether he likes them or dislikes them, whether he is confident or afraid, or whether he is glad to be there or wishes he were somewhere else. The storyteller should like his audience. If the storyteller tells a story to listeners he doesn't like, they will receive the feeling that he doesn't like them. The storyteller should be more concerned about his listeners than about giving a performance.

The storyteller also expresses attitudes as a part of telling his story. He expresses his attitude about each event and each character in the story.

Each story expresses attitudes, feelings and emotions. A story may express a positive or negative attitude. Resignation, cynicism, hostility, shock, horror, sorrow, pain, love, joy, surprise and wonder are some of the attitudes expressed through stories.

The storyteller needs to determine the attitudes he wishes to express. Then he needs to feel those attitudes when telling it. He should not try to act out an attitude. He should work on feeling the attitude he wishes to portray. This will result in his portraying those feelings naturally while telling the story. When the storyteller feels joy, joy will show ho his face. When he feels sad, sadness will show on his face. If he is going to tell a story of hope, he needs to feel hope in his heart.

When the storyteller feels the attitude, the story-listeners will feel it as well. When the teller feels the attitude, he uses his whole body to relate it to his listeners. A prevailing attitude will be expressed by the story as a whole, but each individual event in the sequence has its own distinct attitude.

7. Feedback from the listeners

The listeners' body language gives feedback that helps guide the storyteller. The ability to tell a story and watch one's listeners' reactions helps the storyteller regulate the use of vocal modulation, silence, pause, and speed. The storyteller does his best when he is observing and reacting to his audience.

The listeners' faces help edit the story as it is being told. Happy faces, puzzled faces, confused faces, or shocked faces advise the storyteller to continue as planned, or to make adaptions. Adaptation is natural in storytelling. The storyteller refines or changes his language and delivery in response to the listeners' reaction. The storyteller will discover that his listeners' body language helps shape the story and helps him do a better and clearer job of narrating his story. The storyteller who looks at his listeners receives feedback and knows when he needs to adapt his presentation in order to better communicate.

8. Words

Words put together and spoken out loud weave the story

Story Crafting

together. Words that have cultural significance for both the storyteller and the story-listeners are essential to storytelling. Words are a critical element in storytelling. Just as glass is a medium for light and air a medium for sound, spoken words are a medium for storytelling.

The storyteller will choose the words to be spoken when he is crafting his original story, or he will find them in the existing story he decides to tell.

Story Crafting

PREPARING TO TELL THE STORY

The storyteller needs to prepare in advance. The following suggestions will help the storyteller prepare in advance for the telling his story.

1. **Read the story text numerous times**

    If the story is in written form, the story text needs to be read, reread, reread, and reread. Read your story text silently numerous times. Then read it aloud several times. Keep reading the story until you can recall the sequence of events with a fair amount of accuracy.

    If you crafted your own story and only wrote out the story structure and sequence of events, then read, reread and reread your notes.

2. **Understand the structure of the story**

    Telling a story is similar to flying an airplane. If one knows how to take off and how to land, he can usually find the way to his destination. If the storyteller knows the initial-situation with the initial-problem that begins the story and he knows the final-situation that ends the story, he can remember most of the events that happened along the way.

    People who are good at telling jokes have both the beginning hook sentence and the punch line in mind before telling the joke. The storyteller needs to have in mind both how the story begins and how it ends.

    While telling a tale, the storyteller should not mention the words:

key-character, character's story-goal, key-location, initial-problem, key-attitudes, nor key-repetitions. However, once the storyteller is aware of these things, he is on the road to being prepared to tell his story.

3. **Understand the story from each character's perspective**

    If the storyteller can relate to the characters' point of view, personality, situation, motivation, or actions, he will communicate deeper meaning from the story. It would be helpful for the storyteller to fill out the character perspective chart noting information on each of the prominent characters in the story.

CHARACTER PERSPECTIVE CHART		
KEY CHARACTER	**2nd CHARACTER**	**3rd CHARACTER**
Name of Character	Name of Character	Name of Character
Character's key-problem	Character's key-problem	Character's key-problem

Preparing to Tell the Story

Character's story-goal: What does he/she want?	Character's story-goal: What does he/she want?	Character's story-goal: What does he/she want?
Action: What does he/she do to solve the problem or reach the goal?	Action: What does he/she do to solve the problem or reach the goal?	Action: What does he/she do to solve the problem or reach the goal?
Consequence: What happened as a result of the action?	Consequence: What happened as a result of the action?	Consequence: What happened as a result of the action?

Story Crafting

4. Prepare for several days in advance before telling the story

The storyteller should refer to the structure of his story on a daily basis for many days before the telling of the story. Each day review the initial-situation, the initial-problem, the sequence of events and the final-situation. If the story is written out, he should read the story again, and again, and again.

In order to have a story firmly in memory, the storyteller should repeat it in his mind on a regular basis. In order to retain it, the storyteller must rethink, rethink, and rethink the narrative.

5. Avoid memorizing the story

Many beginning storytellers prepare to tell a story by memorizing the words used to tell the story. They repeat the story, word for word, over and over. Memorization is hard on the storyteller and on the listeners. It is more effective to think, rethink, rethink, and rethink the story; rather than mindlessly repeating words!

Memorization for storytelling becomes a hindrance because the teller relies on his memory which has failed him in the past and will fail him in the future. Losing his place and forgetting words can be terrifying. The act of memorizing the story instills the fear of forgetting it. Memorization inhibits and removes freedom and joy from storytelling. Most memorized stories sound like they were chipped out of granite.

Memorization limits flexibility. The teller needs to adapt stories for different audiences. The teller may show up expecting adult listeners, and discover that half of his audience is composed of children and youth. He needs to make quick adaptations. A memorized story cannot be adapted.

Memorization also produces fear in the listeners. Once listeners realize that the storyteller is reciting lines that were memorized, they start to worry if he is going to make it through to the end. Every pause presents the unsettling possibility that the storyteller has forgotten lines in the story.

Memorization makes the teller word-focused instead of people-focused. The teller becomes focused on making sure his words are correct instead of observing the responses of people who are listening to him.

5.1 Exception: Certain types of stories need to be memorized

The great exception to, "Do not memorize," is literary tales. They have an author and are copyrighted. Ethics dictate that the storyteller does his best to tell the story exactly as the author wrote it.

Some types of stories that need to be memorized:
- Poetic stories
- Ballads (the musical equivalent of literary tales)
- Stories with a rhythmical language structure
- Literary stories that need to honor the copyright version of the author
- Stories crafted by another storyteller and their permission-to-tell requires an identical-text delivery

5.2 Key parts of the story need to be memorized

A guideline for the storyteller: do not memorize the entire story. However, it is helpful to memorize the beginning, the final-situation, essential chants, songs and phrases that are repeated, and lists contained within the story.

Memorize the opening sentences in order to know how to begin. Memorize the final-situation to know how to end the story. That keeps the storyteller from fumbling for a way to get out of the story. Memorizing the initial-situation and the final-situation help the storyteller start strong and end strong.

Essential chants, songs, and phrases that are repeated throughout the story should be memorized. For example, in the story "The Three Little Pigs," each little pig built a house. The wolf knocked on each little pig's door and said, "Little pig, little pig, let me come in." Each little pig answered, "No, no, not by the hair of my chinny chin

chin, I will not let you come in." Each time the wolf answered, "Then I'll huff and I'll puff and I'll blow your house in." Those repeated phrases need to be memorized.

If the storyteller substituted the little pig's answer, "No, no, not by the hair of my chinny chin chin," with, "Not by my whiskers," the story would not work. Essential chants, songs, and phrases should be memorized.

If a story contains a list, it will need to be memorized. For example, the Old Testament Bible story of the Israelites' exodus from Egypt contains a list of ten plagues. To be accurate, the storyteller needs to memorize the list of the plagues.

6. **Visualize and imagine the story before telling it**

Before telling the story of "The Three Bears," the storyteller should visualize, imagine and experience the sensory details of the story. The kitchen scene will come alive for his listeners if the teller has seen the kitchen for himself. In his mind he has seen the bowls the bears use. He has seen their table and knows where they sit. He knows if the kitchen is bright or dingy. His mind has experienced the kitchen and he knows if last night's dishes are piled precariously in the sink, or if they have been organized inside the kitchen cabinet. He may have seen Baby Bear's pictures held up on the refrigerator with people magnets.

For a story to come alive, the teller must "see" the story taking place in his imagination, in the same way that he experiences a dream. The storyteller can imagine things and people that do not exist, and he can experience them as if they were real. The storyteller who uses his imagination to experience his story is ready to convey the sense of vitality to his listeners. To do this, the storyteller needs to use his own imagination to help him understand what happened, to experience the emotions of the story and to communicate them without being theatrical. Using the imagination beforehand helps the storyteller vibrate with emotions while telling the story.

The storyteller needs to use his imagination to mentally virtualize the story he will be telling:

- Sights
- Sounds
- Smells
- Tastes
- Physical sensations
- Emotions
- Intuitions

If the story takes place on the creek bank, the storyteller must see the green grass, the flowers, and the trees. He must feel the wind on his cheeks and in his hair. He must smell the flowers, the pollen, and the damp earth. He must hear the water running over the rocks, the trees rustling, the birds singing, the bees buzzing, and the insects humming. He must taste the cool water and berries along the side of the creek. He must fear the red ants, the mosquitoes, and the snakes hidden under the bushes.

If the story mentions fresh bread coming out of a wood burning cast iron stove, the teller needs to feel the heat from the stove and smell the bread. If the teller is going to tell about a monster, he needs to mentally see it and be afraid of it.

The storyteller uses his imagination in order to understand what happened and to feel the emotions of the story. He must find his way to the center of each character and experience each event from the character's point of view. Before telling the story of "The Three Bears," the storyteller should experience each event from each of the viewpoint of each of the characters – Goldilocks, Mama Bear, Papa Bear and Baby Bear. The more the story is internalized, imagined, and felt, the easier it is to remember details and feel the proper attitudes when it is time to tell the story to listeners.

The storyteller should virtually experience the story with his

Story Crafting

senses and intuition. He won't need to describe all the details to his listeners. The fact that he has experienced the story with his whole body will make his body and voice do amazing things that are subtle, and will help his listeners experience the story with him.

7.   Prepare a story-board to map out the story

A story-board is a visual depiction of the sequence of major events in a story. Each sketch represents an event in the story. Together they depict the story's sequence of events and provide a visual map of the story. The sketches don't need to be a work of art, they can be stick drawings.

Mapping out the story on a sheet of paper with simple sketches helps a storyteller visualize and remember it. Instead of writing words and sentences, the storyteller represents each event of the story with a sketch or stick line drawing. He begins making visual designs for the initial-situation, another for the initial-problem, continues with sketches for each of the major sequence of events, and finishes with a drawing for the final-situation. At times the story-board may include a word or phrase; however, it is mostly simple sketches or stick drawings.

If the storyteller needs notes to help him narrate his story, he uses the visual story-board. He avoids notes using words and phrases, because line drawings help him visualize in his mind each event of the story.

8.   Pantomime the story

Pantomiming is an excellent tool for learning a story without memorizing it. Pantomiming the story to himself helps the storyteller to experience his story with his entire body.

I have been in countries where I did not speak the language. On several occasions I was able to communicate to a sales person by pantomiming and was able to understand the sales person who pantomimed to me. To buy eggs, I put my fingers from my two hands together to form an oval shape. Then I put my hands under my arm pits and flapped my arms as if they were wings, and I clucked like a chicken.

The pantomimic communicates through bodily movement instead of the spoken word. To express by pantomime is to communicate a thought, action, object, or event by means of bodily movements, gestures, facial expressions and attitudes. For example, one would pantomime the idea of a "baby" by cradling an imaginary infant.

To pantomime a story, the storyteller practices the story without using his voice. However, as he practices, he will use the full range of movement allowed by the human body to express each thought, attitude, dialogue, object, and event found in the story.

I suggest that the storyteller pantomime the story to himself in two stages:

1st <u>First stage</u>: While reading the story or going over the sequence of events, use gestures and facial expression to express each event in the story.

2nd <u>Second stage</u>: Remember the details of the story without memorizing it. At this point, minimize the spoken word by saying few words while concentrating on pantomiming each event and dialogue with gestures and body movement.

Pantomiming the story builds up muscle memory and enables the teller to remember the story without memorizing it.

9. Rehearse the story

The storyteller should practice telling his story out loud. Rehearsing helps him know which parts come easily and which need more work. Rehearsing helps him know if he has all the facts in mind. Telling the story out loud helps fix the story in his mind and gives him opportunity to work on his voice and gestures.

When my wife and I lived on a farm, I often would tell the story to our Lab Retriever, or to one of my horses. Now we live in a town

Story Crafting

and as I take a walk or run a slow jog, I rehearse the story out loud. Sometimes I drop in on a friend at his office. He always takes time to listen to my story. Many storytellers rehearse the story by telling it to a family member.

The storyteller should take time to tell the story out loud. He may want to tell it several times. He should practice, practice, practice. Practice doesn't make perfect; however, it helps to create and improve storytelling habits.

Each time the storyteller rehearses the story, he needs to mentally experience every detail. He needs to make sure he is seeing, feeling, smelling, tasting, and hearing everything. He must build empathy toward each character and smell them, see them, hear them, observe their mannerisms and their postures, and feel their moods and emotions. The more the storyteller mentally experiences everything, the more his listeners will experience the story.

The storyteller should always rehearse as if someone were listening to him. He should visualize an audience. As he rehearses, he will fine tune his gestures, and his voice, rate, pitch, volume levels and qualities. His mentally experiencing the story each time he tells it will do much of this fine tuning for him.

10. Utilize the sequence of events in telling the story

Storytelling is a natural process. Start with the initial-situation and the initial-problem, continue with the sequence of events, and end with the final-situation.

11. Making mistakes is a reality

The only places where perfect people exist are in books and films. The reason is that the mistakes are edited out. In the storytelling world, the storyteller must speak without an editor to remove his errors. And he will make mistakes. Those willing to err are the only ones who will improve. The best plan to improve one's storytelling abilities is to tell stories, tell stories, and tell more stories. Keep telling stories and the mind will become sharper at remembering details. The one who constantly tells stories will never become perfect; however, he will constantly improve.

12. Trust the story

The storyteller should tell the story with confidence. Stories impact the lives of both the storyteller and the listeners. Trust the story! The storyteller can trust the story to produce results beyond his expectations. One can never predict the results of a well-told story, but the storyteller should expect the results to surprise him with joy.

Story Crafting

WARM-UP BEFORE STORYTELLING

A fellow storyteller reviewed this book and asked me, "Why are you including the chapter on warm-ups?" She didn't see a need for this chapter.

I've done public speaking, classroom teaching, and storytelling for more than forty years. Throughout the years I've had a problem with coughing while I was speaking. I always had cough drops in my mouth when speaking. When I was sixty-six years old, I took a graduate course in storytelling performance. Before students would tell stories in class, our professor led us in fifteen minutes of warm-ups. I observed that when I did light exercises and stretching before speaking, I had no problem with coughing. I experimented with doing warm-ups before storytelling, speaking or preaching, and I was freed from my usual problem with coughing. I researched articles on doing warm-ups for actors and musicians and developed this material for myself to use.

I've observed several professional storytellers stretching and warming-up before performing. I know one who claims to take an hour and half to warm-up before performing. However, many do not feel the need to do warm-ups.

The voice is an invaluable storytelling tool and the storyteller must protect it like a football quarterback protects the ball. The storyteller should protect his voice like a professional violinist protects her instrument. Professional athletes always warm up before the beginning of each game. The storyteller should protect his voice by warming-up before a performance.

I don't warm-up before telling a short story to a few friends sitting in our den nor to tell a five-minute story to a small group. However, I need to warm up when I must project my voice over a length of time. I often do the breathing and voice warm-ups when I am driving to a speaking or storytelling engagement, and after arriving at my destination, I try to find a private place where I can do stretching exercises.

These warm-ups have 3 basic principles behind them:

1st   Stretching

2nd   Proper breathing

3rd   Warming up the voice gently before intensive use

STRETCHING

There is a right way and a wrong way to stretch. The right way is a relaxed, sustained stretch while focusing your attention on the muscle being stretched. The wrong way is to bounce up and down, or to stretch to the point of pain. Stretching, when done correctly, stops the stretch before pain is felt. The right way does good; the wrong way can do harm.

I know from experience that the wrong kind of stretch can do damage. I've been a long distance runner since I was twenty-four. A fellow runner showed me a stretching exercise that I have been using for years. One day, when I was sixty seven years old, while stretching, I felt a popping sensation in my left knee joint. I experienced a meniscal tear and surgery was required to repair it. I showed the stretch I had been doing to my orthopaedic doctor, and he said, "That stretch is good for my business but bad for my patients."

Do easy stretches. Stretch to the point where you feel a mild tension, then relax as you hold the stretch for 10-30 seconds.

1.   **Stretches for the back, shoulders and arms**

   1.1   With the palms together, extend the arms overhead.

Story Crafting

Stretch arms upward and slightly backwards. Hold the stretch for 10-15 seconds. This is a great stretch for the muscles of the outer portions of the arms, shoulders and ribs.

1.2 Place the left wrist on the right shoulder. With the right hand, grasp the left elbow and gently pull it across your chest toward your right shoulder. Hold stretch for 10-15 seconds. Now do the same thing with the right elbow. This will stretch your shoulder and the middle of the upper back.

1.3 Cross the arms and then put them over the head. Hold the elbow of one arm with the hand of the other arm. Gently and slowly pull the elbow behind your head, creating a stretch. Hold the stretch for 15-20 seconds. Now stretch the other side. This is a stretch for the triceps and the top of your shoulders.

1.4 Interlace your fingers behind your back. Slowly turn your elbows inward while straightening your arms. Then lift your arms up behind until you feel a stretch in the arms, shoulders or chest. Hold the stretch for 10-20 seconds.

2. **Stretch for the lower back, hips, and hamstrings**

Start in a standing position with feet about shoulder width apart and pointed straight ahead. Bend your knees slightly. Slowly bend forward from the hips. Let your neck and arms relax. Go to the point where you feel a slight stretch in the back of your legs. Do not stretch with knees locked or bounce when you stretch. Stretch for 20-30 seconds. Keep your knees bent when you stand up.

3. **Stretches for the upper body**

   3.1 Extend both arms overhead. Grasp your right hand with your left hand and bend slowly to the left, using your left arm to gently pull the right arm over the head and down toward the ground. Come out of the stretch slowly and then stretch to the right. Hold each stretch for 10-20 seconds.

3.2 Stand about 18 inches away from a wall with your back towards it. With your feet about shoulder width apart and toes pointed straight ahead, slowly turn your upper body around until you can place your hands on the wall at about shoulder height. Hold stretch for 20-30 seconds. Return to the starting position, and then turn in the opposite direction and touch the wall and stretch.

4. **Stretches for the face and neck**

    4.1 Begin to stretch the neck by allowing your head to fall forward gently as if you had no neck. Very slowly rotate you head to the right; do not force it all the way back. Reverse and slowly rotate your head to the left. Be careful that you do this gently, with no jarring or jerky movements.

    4.2 Stretch your face by raising your eyebrows and opening you eyes as wide as possible. At the same time, open your mouth as wide as you can and stick your tongue out as far as you can. Hold for 5-10 seconds. Then with your eyebrows raised and eyes wide open, force the biggest grin possible and hold for 5-10 seconds.

BREATHING WARM-UPS

Be conscious of how you breathe. Deep breathing is essential for safe, healthy, effective voice production. When you breathe in, aim to feel as if you take in air as low down in your body as possible without your shoulders having to rise. Allow stomach muscles to relax outwards as you breathe in.

When you speak, your navel should move towards your backbone. If this doesn't happen, you won't get the best from your voice and you may even damage your voice without realizing it. Look for this in the breathing exercises below.

1. **Inhale deeply**

    Put one hand on your abdomen and the other on your stomach

beneath the sternum. Inhale deeply without moving the upper chest and shoulders.

Practice panting like a dog.

2. Inhale and exhale slowly and deeply

Inhale slowly through the nose for a count of 10 and exhale slowly through the mouth for a count of 10.

3. Introduce humming to exhaling

Humming is one of the best ways to warm up or cool down the vocal cords.

4. Introduce vocalization to exhaling

Inhale deeply, pick a comfortable pitch, and while exhaling, produce the vowel sound "ah". With other breath, practice increasing and decreasing the volume sound of "ah."

Inhale deeply and exhale slowly while making an "s" sound. Hold the "s" sound steady for as long as possible on one breath.

WARMING-UP THE VOICE GENTLY BEFORE INTENSIVE USE

1. Exercises for an open throat

   1.1 Stimulate the area where the skull meets the vertebral column

   With the middle three fingers of each hand, gently massage the area on each side of the spinal column. Gently massage the area where you feel little balls of muscle until the balls are minimized.

   1.2 Light exercises to loosen up

   Rotate both shoulders together five times.

   Lift the shoulders up to the ears and drop them. Do this five times.

1.3 Yawn

Do several yawns; then do vocalized yawns by introducing vibrations of the vocal folds with the "ah" sound. Keep the throat and jaws relaxed.

2. Exercises for articulation

2.1 Exercises for the lips

2.1.1 Smile-pucker
Do an exaggerated smile; show your teeth and draw your lips as tightly as possible. Say, "eeeeeeeeeee." Then exaggerate protruding your lips to make a pucker and say "ooooooooo." Alternate between doing a smile and a pucker.

2.1.2 Do exaggerated lip movements
Do exaggerated lip movement as you say:

- In Spain it rains mainly in the plains; in Spain it rains mainly in the plains.
- Tea for two, tea for two, tea for two, tea for two, tea for two, tea for two.
- Free fruit, free fruit, free fruit, free fruit, free fruit.
- Wee-way, wee-way, wee-way, wee-way, wee-way.
- Which witch is which, which witch is which, which witch is which?

3. Exercises for the jaw

3.1 Massage the jaw muscles

Use your fingertips and gently massage the jaw muscles with up and down strokes.

Relax your jaw, allowing it to drop and open your mouth. Move the relaxed jaw from left to right with your hand.

3.2 Say silly phrases

Each phrase features different difficult consonant combinations. Start slow, over-articulating and then increase speed.

Story Crafting

- The tip of the tongue, the lips, the teeth
- Red letter, yellow letter
- Good blood, bad blood
- Really rural
- Unique New York
- It's awfully difficult for the tolerant to tolerate the intolerant
- Saw logs, saw logs, saw logs, saw logs, saw logs
- See-saw, see-saw, see-saw, see-saw, see-saw, see-saw
- Cars and bars mean stars and scars. Cars and bars mean stars and scars
- Law me, Law me, law me, law me, law me, law me
- The stronger sex is the weaker sex because the weakness of the stronger sex is the strength of the weaker sex.

3.3 Say tongue twisters

A tongue twisters is a phrase or sentence which is hard to speak fast, usually because of alliteration or a sequence of nearly similar sounds. It helps develop speech skills.

These long tongue twister contains many buzz sounds and difficult consonant combinations. It is possible to say all in one breath if you use diaphragmatic breathing and carefully control the volume of air expelled. Articulate every sound!

1) What a to-do to die today at a minute or two to two,
   a thing distinctly hard to say but harder still to do.
   For they'll beat a tattoo at a quarter to two:
   a rat-ta tat-tat ta tat-tat ta to-to.
   And the dragon will come when he hears the drum
   at a minute or two to two today, at a minute or two to two.

2) Peter Piper picked a peck of pickled peppers.
   Did Peter Piper pick a peck of pickled peppers?
   If Peter Piper picked a peck of pickled peppers,
   where's the peck of pickled peppers Peter Piper picked?

3) Betty Botter had some butter,
   "But," she said, "this butter's bitter.
   If I bake this bitter butter,
   it would make my batter bitter.
   But a bit of better butter--
   would make my batter better."
   So she bought a bit of butter,
   better than her bitter butter,
   and she baked it in her batter,
   and the batter was not bitter.
   So 'twas better Betty Botter
   bought a bit of better butter.

4) How much wood would a woodchuck chuck
   if a woodchuck could chuck wood?
   He would chuck, he would, as much wood as he could,
   and chuck as much wood as a woodchuck could
   if a woodchuck could chuck wood.

To get the full effect of a short tongue twister you should repeat it several times, as quickly as possible, without stumbling or mispronouncing. Say each of the following tongue twisters slowly, clearly articulating all consonants and vowels. Then say each one quickly four times, maintaining clear articulation of all speech sounds.

- Sweet Sally Sue sat by the sea shore selling sea shells to sea sick sailors.
- Tom Tucker the terrible teacher taught two tots naughty thoughts.
- Much whirling water makes the mill wheel work well.
- Tim the teetotaler took taut twine to tie ten twigs to two tall trees.

OTHER VOCAL HEALTH HINTS

1. While performing, be sure you keep your vocal folds moist

Story Crafting

and well lubricated. You can do this by drinking plenty of liquids throughout the storytelling performance.

2. Keep caffeine consumption (tea, coffee, and soft drinks) to a minimum, because caffeine dries out the vocal folds and can make the voice sound raspy and scratchy. Do not drink alcohol before a performance because it dehydrates the body and therefore, the vocal folds.

3. After speaking for a long time, warm-down by drinking some tepid water or caffeine free warm tea. Yawn and then breathe deeply.

4. Look after your voice. Don't strain it. If possible, eliminate background noise instead of speaking loudly over it. If you need to project your voice in order to be heard, use diaphragmatic breathing and carefully control the volume of air expelled.

PROTECTING YOUR VOICE WHEN YOU BECOME HOARSE OR HAVE A SORE THROAT

The storyteller wakes up on the day of a big performance and he feels a sore throat or he is hoarse. What does he do? If the sore throat is due to an infection, it will take a couple of days for antibiotics to begin healing. If he is just hoarse, no cure exists for a hoarse throat, just recovery, and that takes time.

Doctors and voice coaches would advice him, "When you feel the slightest indication of hoarseness coming on, cancel your speaking engagements. Try to avoid any speaking for a day or two. Do not even whisper."

Often the storyteller is determined to go ahead with his performance. The following are suggestions that have helped some storytellers, public speakers and singers:

- Gargle the throat with cayenne pepper tea (a half teaspoon of cayenne pepper to a hot cup of water).
- Fold a towel and pour rubbing alcohol onto it. Wrap the wet

- side of the towel around the throat and keep it there for about 30 minutes. Repeat every four hours.

- Take a capsule of pro-biotic, open the capsule and place the powder as deep into the throat as possible. Wait as long as possible before swallowing. Repeat two or three times a day. Pro-biotic can be found at natural health stores.

- Avoid loud speaking. Speak softly, use the microphone, and depend on the sound system to project your voice.

The storyteller needs to be aware that abusing his voice when he has a sore throat or is hoarse, may result in damaging his voice. I once took classes with a man who was an ex-pastor. One Sunday, the pastor awoke with a sore throat. He forced himself to preach twice that Sunday; however, that was the last time he preached. He damaged his vocal cords to the extent that he was unable to project his voice. The ex-pastor returned to school to prepare for a career where he would not need to use his voice.

The storyteller who is having difficulty with his voice on performance day, should ask himself this question, "Is this event so important that I am going to perform even if it means that I will never tell another story in public?"

Story Crafting

LISTENING IMPROVES STORYTELLING

A child stands in front of dad, bursting to tell him about the goal he made in soccer. However, dad has the paper in front of his face and a ball game is on TV. Dad looks over the paper at his son, but at the same time he glances at the ball game on TV. Dad is not listening to his son while he is multiple-tasking. Dad needs to listen with his ears and his eyes. In today's world, people work at tuning out much of the information that is thrust at them. It is important for the storyteller to change from being a deflector to becoming a receiver, much like a satellite dish.

Storytellers must develop the skill of listening. Hearing is different than listening. The ability to hear is typically innate, but the ability to listen is an acquired skill that must be developed and practiced. Listening involves paying attention and making a conscious effort to process what is heard and observed. Listening is different than hearing friends, co-workers, or family talking over lunch. That kind of hearing is usually done while thinking about how to respond. It takes concentration and determination to become a good listener. The storyteller should be deliberate with his listening and remind himself constantly that his goal is to truly hear what speakers are saying and observe the way they are saying it.

The storyteller needs to listen to the rhythms and music of language. He discerns the formal from the colloquial, and characteristics that make each speaker unique.

The storyteller without listening skills will have all his story-characters reflecting his own speaking habits. All his story-characters will speak similar to each other. He'll have doctors and lawyers, farmers and bankers, men and women, Yankees and Southerners, children and adults – all speaking the same way. A story doesn't sound authentic if all characters speak the same way.

The storyteller should develop the habit of listening to people who surround him. Go to the mall, sit on a bench, and listen to shoppers. When eating at a fast food restaurant, listen to the chatter of others. Eavesdrop on total strangers. Listen to nearby people as they talk on the cell phone. While eavesdropping, listen to environmental sounds. Hear the percolator gurgling up the coffee, the music in the background, sound of glasses and silverware rattling in the restaurant, the hum of the air conditioner, the whine of tires on a nearby street, and the click of the computer keys on the nearby laptop.

The storyteller should listen with his eyes as well as his ears. Sit on a bench and watch people. Some people are attractive; others are not. Some people seem peculiar; others are so anonymous that they're almost invisible. Watch how people move. Everyone has a unique walk. Everyone uses his hands in a unique way. Some people throw their heads back when they laugh; others lower their chins and chuckle into their chests. Watch how people talk. Some people hold their heads still while talking; others bob their heads constantly. Watch what people do with their legs when they sit down.

The storyteller who watches people will find real-live models to imitate when he portrays a story-character. The storyteller can flip through mental-file-cards of people he has observed when figuring out how a character should walk, stand or talk. Everything observed becomes a part of that memory bank that will be drawn upon in portraying story-characters.

The storyteller who improves his listening skills will improve his storytelling skills. Here are some suggestions to help improve listening skills. They are not in any order of importance.

Story Crafting

1. **Practice intentional listening**

   When in a group, the storyteller should make the choice to listen and observe without responding to every speaker. It is difficult to receive information when the mind is working on how to respond. The intentional listener doesn't silently argue with the speaker or judge his remarks; he concentrates on observing and understanding the speaker. He listens to the speaker's words and observes his body language. Intentional listening prevents the listener from thinking about how he will respond. His focus is listening with his ears and eyes. He watches facial expressions, gestures and postures. He observes if the speaker is leaning forward or backward. He observes the gestures he makes with his hands.

   To reproduce storytelling dialogue, the storyteller must observe characteristics of speakers, such as:

   - Physical idiosyncrasies (pulling earlobe, rubbing nose, etc.)
   - Speech accent and dialect (foreign, southern, northern, south western, etc.)
   - Distinguished vocal characteristics (pitch variety, volume, breathy, thin, flat, nasal, tense, throaty, deep rich sound, rate)
   - Speech characteristics (flattering, blunt, sharp, rude, polished, etc.)
   - Speech idiosyncrasies (constantly clearing throat, speaking from side of mouth, etc.)
   - Speech addictions (murmuring "un-hum," or constantly repeating a word, etc.)
   - Catch phrases (expressions like "Oh dear," that keep reappearing)

2. **Face the speaker**

   A good listener looks at the speaker. The listener's eyes help complete the communication circuit that needs to be established between speaker and listener. A listener should focus on the speaker's mouth, eyes, and hands. He should face the speaker, watch his eyes, and resist the urge to think about how he wants to respond. He should concentrate on hearing the words and watching body language. A good listener is similar to a poor boxer. A good boxer keeps his face covered. A poor boxer, like a good listener, leaves his face open.

3. Avoid distractions

My wife often enters my office to talk to me and she asks me to put my laptop on standby and close it, or put any open book face down on my desk. A good listener avoids distractions and gives the speaker undivided attention. In order to listen, get rid of any distraction: close a book, turn off the TV, close the laptop, and ignore the ringing cell phone.

4. Pay attention to non-verbal communications

A good listener observes what is said through pauses, silence, unspoken words and body language. He observes body language: a raised eye brow, a side-ways glance, twitching hands, or shuffling feet. He discerns what the speaker is saying with unspoken words. A good listener observes if the sound of the speaker's voice fits the body language. Is the voice soft and gracious, but the hands are formed into tight fists? Is the voice cheerful but the face stern?

5. Respond actively

The listener should make a conscious effort to hear spoken words and send signals that the message is being received. He can respond with a simple nod of the head or a voiced "uh huh." These responses don't signal agreement, but indicates listening. The listener can respond by recapping or summarizing the speaker's comments with as few words as possible. Such response sends signals to the speaker and keeps the listener's mind from wandering. The listener should ask leading questions to clarify or obtain more information, without giving his own opinion.

Examples of a listener recapping a speakers words:

Story Crafting

Speaker: "Yesterday, I was in the stockroom working. Boss left. Phone rang. I let it ring. Boss never told me to answer it. He returned and blamed me for losing him a sale. Today, boss went to lunch. Phone rang. I answered. It was his wife. Now he's mad because his wife knows he ate out instead of eating the diet lunch she fixed. How was I to know it was his wife?"

Listener: "Your boss sends you mixed signals."

The storyteller needs to work on improving his listening skills in order to improve his storytelling skills. It is essential to develop good listening and observation skills if he is to craft authentic sounding dialogue. He must develop listening and observation skills in order to portray characters who appear authentic to his audience.

Story Crafting

CHILDREN AND STORYTELLING

Most of my storytelling has been to audiences that include all age groups – children, youth and adults. Children are usually present when I tell my stories, but they don't make up most of the audiences. I have done some storytelling to children. My wife was a kindergarten and first-grade teacher, and has taught children in church from the time she was twelve years old. She has lots of experience telling stories to children and I depend on her to advise me when I am preparing to tell stories to children. I developed some guidelines to help me when I'm preparing to tell stories to children.

A good story will appeal to many age groups. I have told stories for an adult audience where children were present. The children listened and participated. Some folk tales, fairy tales, multi-cultural stories and personal stories appeal to all ages.

Children respond differently in an audience that include all age groups than they do in a single-age audience. Young teenagers in an audience with just teenagers might reject a story as being too babyish. However, if children and family members are present, they would love the story and freely participate.

One big difference in telling stories to children, rather than adults, is that younger children let the storyteller know how he is doing. If they don't like his stories, they will squirm, interrupt, or get up and leave. If they like his stories, they get comfortable and gaze at the storyteller in rap adoration. However, older elementary and adolescent audiences may not give transparent feedback. They try to hide all expressions of enthusiasm from their peers. Adolescents love storytelling as much as preschoolers – they simply don't show it

Story Crafting

the way younger children do.

Children spend a lot of time using their imagination. Therefore, it is easy for children to travel to the imaginary story world.

1. Characteristics common to children's stories

Three common characteristics found in stories loved by children are: quick action and lots of action, familiar things involved in doing something that is unfamiliar, and repetition.

1.1 Action

Children love stories where every sequence of events tells what story-characters did or what they said. Almost no time is spent in explanation, description or telling how the characters felt. In children's stories, the events follow one after another in time, with one action causing another. Children's stories should not have spin-offs which require a return to the main story-line.

1.2 Start with the familiar and move to the unfamiliar

The stories need to be about familiar, concrete things that can be seen, heard, tasted, felt or touched. However, something needs to be different or strange about those familiar things. To take a child to a story world, start with material that is common to the world they know, but give it a difference. Create a story world out of material from the world they know.

Each object or character in the story presents a distinct picture to the imagination, and these pictures are made out of very simple elements with which the children are familiar. Each object, character, and happening is very much like everyday, yet touched with a subtle difference. For example, the details of the "The Three Bears" story are parts of everyday life – house, chairs, beds, and so on. Yet something is different; they are the house, chairs, and beds of three bears. That is the touch of marvel which transforms the scene. "The Three Little Pigs" story starts with things common to everyday life – mother, children, straw, wood and brick. Yet the difference is that the characters are not people – they are pigs and a wolf who talk and act like people.

1.3 Repetition

A degree of repetition is found in most children's stories. Words, chants, songs, phrases, themes, patterns, actions, facts or ideas are repeated, either exactly or with minor variations. For example, in the story of "The Three Little Pigs," each little pig built a house, the wolf knocked on each little pig's door and said, "Little pig, little pig, let me come in." Each little pig answered, ""No, no, not by the hair of my chinny chin chin; I will not let you come in." Each time the wolf answered, "Then I'll huff and I'll puff and I'll blow your house in." Those repeated phrases help children remember and love the story.

When you are looking for stories to tell children, apply this threefold test as a kind of touchstone to their quality of fitness: Are they full of action? Are they about things that children know about? Is repetition built into the story?

2. Guidelines for different ages

The ages of children, who are the primary audience, should impact the kind of stories the storyteller chooses to tell. When telling stories to mixed ages, select most of the stories so they will be understood by the younger children in the audience. Each story should be appropriate for everyone present, even if some things may require explanation for the youngest listeners to understand. Keep each story under ten minutes so the youngest listeners aren't left out of a story for long. Make sure all stories are entertaining to older children and adults present, and would be easy for them to explain to younger children later. Do not tell stories with content that adults would not want to discuss with their children on the ride home.

Children, like adults, should be exposed to many different types of stories. Many folktales, fairy tales, legends, myths, personal stories, and tall tales are perfect for children of all ages.

All age groups like stories about people their age. Children also like stories about those who are one or two years older than they are.

Story Crafting

The following guidelines can help the teller find stories for certain age group audiences.

2.1 The 3-6 year-olds: Age of Repetition

This age group loves stories that are about concrete things that can be seen, smelled, touched, felt, heard, and tasted. They like stories that tell about familiar objects, animals that talk, and a lot of repetition in the sequence of events. They like stories about other children their own age.

Things that children experience and like to do are effective when included in the story. Remember, children like to get dirty, splash in puddles, play with an adult around, try something new for the first time, etc.

Most younger children want to hear the same story repeated many times. They need to hear a story many times in order to master it. If you do repeat performances to the same children, be prepared to repeat the children's favorite stories on several occasions

For preschool children, physical participation may be necessary to ensure the children's attention for more than a few minutes. Their bodies are growing rapidly; therefore, they physically cannot sit still for very long. Sometimes little children will listen to a quiet story, but if they are restless, participation is the surest route to engage them in your story.

Chose stories with only one plot. Such stories will not use words similar to: "meanwhile" or "while that was happening."

Sample Stories:
- Dr Seuss stories
- The Little Red Hen
- If You Give a Mouse a Cookie
- Alexander and the Terrible, Horrible, No Good, Very Bad Day
- Tale of Peter Rabbit
- Stone Soup

2.2 The 6-9 year-olds: Age of Fancy

This age group likes fantasy stories, fables, wonder tales, and folk tales in which good is rewarded and evil is punished.

They enjoy stories that take them to other lands and worlds, and characters who do exciting things.

They like stories about other children their own age who live in far away places and have exciting adventures.

Sample stories:
- Uncle Remus and B'rer Rabbit tales
- The Day Jimmy's Boa Ate the Wash
- Different Fables
- Folk tales

2.3 The 9-12 year-olds: Age of Hero Worship

This age is fascinated with hero worship. They like danger, adventure, and action. They love experiencing the success or failures of heroes and they relish action.

Chose stories with surprising endings and punch lines that challenge their thinking. Stories about a person with a secret, mystery stories, and stories with horses and dogs are popular.

They like stories about children their own age, or one or two years older, who live in far away places and face danger and adventure.

Sample stories:
- Jack stories and other "fool" stories
- Paul Bunyan
- Johnny Appleseed
- Sport stories
- Tall tales about animals are preferred over stories with talking animals

2.4 The 12-18: Age of Idealism

These border-line young adults don't want to listen to stories they feel that they have outgrown. Such stories make them feel childish. If the storyteller chooses to tell a children's story, he should explain his reasons for telling it.

Teenagers continue to like stories that contain adventure, suspense and excitement. Early teen children like stories that contain unusual experiences, surprises or unexpected endings.

Most teenagers like stories about explorations, expeditions, outdoor life and sports. They like stories about children with horses, dogs and other pets.

Middle and older teenagers gravitate toward stories about male-female relationships, romance, family relations, as well as stories that explore vocational or professional areas.

Peer group approval has become essential for older children and youth. Therefore, they are often reluctant to take an adult's suggestion before their peers. Also, adolescents have an aversion to anything they see as "childish" behavior. However, if they are treated as young adults in a non-threatening environment, they will bark like a dog, flap imaginary wings like a bird and yell out answers.

Sample stories that high school students enjoy are:
- Jack London's stories
- Jump tales
- Contemporary (urban) legends
- Stories of justice
- Stories of male-female relationships
- War stories
- Mark Twain stories
- Tall tales

3. **Story length**

A rule of thumb is children have a minute of attention span for each year they have lived. Therefore, the story length should average about a minute for each year of the average age of children who are story-listeners. If the listeners are five years old, the storyteller should tell stories that take less than five minutes to tell. He should tell a story that is five minutes or less, have a participation activity, then tell another story that takes about five minutes.

Longer stories can be told with frequent listener participation. Audience participation activities include children repeating a phrase, giving information, miming action, singing along with a short repetitious song, using hand motions or inviting volunteers to help illustrate the story.

Children love to move, to see things develop in front of them, and they love to yell, talk, laugh, and make themselves part of the story. Participation gets the children's attention and brings them into the story. The younger the listeners, the more active they should be in telling the story. The better the storyteller becomes at including the children's participation, the larger number of children he will be able to captivate at one time.

4.   Be flexible

When the storyteller goes to perform for children, he needs to have a plan in mind, but he needs to be prepared to make adaptations. He arrives with his selected stories and the order he plans to tell them. Yet he needs to be prepared to change his plans during his performance.

Situations the students are facing may require adaptations. Learning that the students are sad because a favorite teacher or classmate is near death, may require dropping or adding a story.

The location may require adaptations. Students seated on a hard wooden floor in a cold gym have a harder time concentrating than those seated on a carpeted floor in a cozy library. The storyteller standing on a stage above and distant from the students faces a different audience than when he is sitting on a chair surrounded by students sitting on the carpet.

The actions and attitudes of adults who are present may require adaptations. The teller faces a different audience when the teachers sit listening to the stories with their students than when the teachers sit in the back of the room correcting homework.

5. Suggestions for problem situations

The storyteller faces a delicate situation when a disruptive child is in the audience. One disruptive child can distract and disrupt a storytelling performance. But if the storyteller tries to discipline the disruptive child, parents may become offended. A parent may calmly watch a disruptive child jump around and distract others. But if the storyteller calls attention to the disruptive child, the parent may feel offended and disrupt the performance by verbally assaulting the storyteller.

Before performing, the storyteller should talk privately to the person in charge and inform him that the storyteller is not the disciplinary person. Be tactful, but inform him that you will depend on the person in charge to deal with any disciplinary problems that could arise. Ask the person(s) in charge to sit with the children and participate in the storytelling event.

When children ask questions, and then keep talking, the storyteller can ask, "What do I give you in exchange for a question?"

(Answer: "You ask me a question and I give you an answer.)

If children keep asking questions, the storyteller can ask, "Do you want me to answer questions or tell you a story? If I answer questions, I won't have time to tell you stories." Or, he may say, "After I tell you my stories, I'll answer your questions."

Suggestions for dealing with disruptive children:

- Sometimes looking directly at a disruptive child or his parents solves the problem.
- The storyteller can request, "Would someone please help this child?"
- The storyteller can call attention, "This child is climbing on stage, I'm afraid he could be hurt. Would his teacher or parent please help him?"

- The storyteller can look at a child and say, "This is not like TV. I can see you."
- The storyteller can compliment other children as he performs. Usually, the disruptive children will behave in order to receive compliments.
- If some children are loud, the storyteller can bend toward those children, look straight at them and speak softly. Children will usually quiet down to hear him.

A technique for getting control of a noisy room is the **If You Can Hear Me** game. An adult stands in front of the children and quietly says, "If you can hear me, put your hands on your head." The adult puts his hands on his head; a few children catch on and begin to play the game. The adult increases the volume of his voice and says, "If you can hear me, pat your stomach." More children join in and the noise dies down. The adult increases his voice level until everyone hears the instruction and follows the action.

It is almost impossible for the storyteller to obtain children's attention in hyper situations. Hyper situations include:

- Children asked to sit quietly after running and playing
- Children who have just eaten are restless due to sugar and caffeine intake, or they are sleepy and have trouble concentrating, because their blood has rushed to the stomach to aid in digestion
- A nearby distraction occurs, such as someone juggling balls, a band warming up or a ball game
- Children are anxious for the main attraction, because Santa Claus or the Easter Bunny is standing nearby with boxes of gifts. If the storyteller is to be followed by Santa Claus or the Easter Bunny, keep them out of sight and avoid mentioning them until the storyteller finishes his performance. Also, the storyteller should not be expected to get the children to settle down and listen to stories after the appearance of Santa Claus, the Easter Bunny or a clown.

Story Crafting

- Refreshments being put on nearby tables will distract children and get them thinking about food

Story Crafting

AUDIENCE PARTICIPATION

Audience participation stories are those where the storyteller engages the audience directly in the telling. Storytelling is an audience-involving art form; the teller can plan activities that result in the teller and the audience co-creating the tales. Setting up audience participation enhances the fun of storytelling, both for the teller and for his listeners.

Audience participation should be a natural part of the story. The storyteller doesn't want the audience to think he invented something for them to do. The activity should fit the story the way a glove fits the hand. Also, the activity should fit the age group of the audience.

Audience participation seems to work best with audiences between the ages of 4-12 and adults. Teenagers seem to have an aversion from adults telling them what to do, and from engaging in behavior they see as "childish."

1. Types of audience participation

Audience participation activities include having listeners repeat a phrase, give information, mime action, sing along with a short repetitious song, use hand motions or ask volunteers to help illustrate the story.

1.1 Repeating phrases

Many stories contain a phrase or refrain that is repeated over and over. When that happens, get the listeners to repeat it with you. Three options for doing this are:

Story Crafting

1st   The storyteller may want to prepare his listeners to repeat a refrain before he tells his tale. He can say something similar to, "I need your help. When I point upwards, say with me, 'Tim can do it. Come on Tim, you can do it!'"

2nd   The storyteller can start telling the story. After repeating a phrase a couple of times, when he comes to it again, he motions with his hands for the listeners to join in.

3rd   Break the audience into antiphonal groups with a story containing multiple repetitious refrains. For example, "The Three Little Pigs" has the refrain spoken by the wolf and the defiant refrain spoken by each of the three little pigs. The storyteller invites half the listeners to huff and puff with the wolf and the other half to shout the little pigs' defiance.

1.2   Requesting information

The storyteller can request information from his listeners. For example, "How many dwarfs did Snow White meet?"

The teller may request information and then weave his listeners answers into his story. I tell the story of Robert who played the trumpet. Robert always took the trumpet with him and imitated the sounds he heard. I could say, "Robert went into the barn. What animal did Robert find in the barn? ... He found a horse. What sound does the horse make? ... Robert played his trumpet making the sound of a horse neighing. What other animal did Robert find in the barn?... He found a cow. What sound does the cow make? ... Robert played his trumpet making the sound of a cow mooing."

1.3   Making sounds

Have the listeners make the sound of a rainstorm by rubbing hands together, next snapping their fingers, and then slapping their hands on their legs. Have the listeners make the sounds of pigs oinking, horses neighing, cows mooing, etc.

1.4 Miming action

Listeners can be asked to mime certain actions related to the story. The storyteller can mime part of the story as he tells it. The he ask his listeners to accompany him by imitating his gestures and body movements. He can have them mime pulling on a rope, walking or running. When he tells about a bird, he can have them mime a bird flying.

The storyteller can play a mime game. For example, the storyteller can throw an imaginary ball to a child in the audience and have the child catch it and throw it back to him. Or he could say, "My dog Shadow won't come. Could you help me call Shadow by snapping your fingers? ... Oh, there's Shadow; would you like to pet him ... reach out and pet him."

1.5 Echoing

Listeners are invited to portray the echo in the story. The storytellers sings or pronounces odd sounds and phrases, and, upon his gesturing to join-in, the audience echoes them back.

1.6 Sing along with a short repetitious song

I have observed several storytellers with musical abilities weave a short song into their story. Each time the song reappears, the listeners join in and sing along.

1.7 Using volunteers

The storyteller can use volunteers to come to the front to help him illustrate the story. For example, the storyteller can tell a story about his pets. He could ask for volunteers and say, "Every time I mention my dog, you bark." He turns to another volunteer and says, "Every time I mention my pet snake, you hiss."

If the teller has objects that illustrate his story, have volunteers hold the objects. When he mentions the object in the story, the volunteer holds it up.

2. Preparing for audience participation

It requires skill for the storyteller to have audience participation. The storyteller needs discipline and technique to make it work. But it is a skill that can be learned by any storyteller. Audience participation begins when the storyteller is preparing his story. He forms a clear picture of the behavior he wants from the audience. Then he makes notes in the story's sequence of events on when and how he plans to invite the listeners to participate in the story.

3. Inform the audience how to participate

The storyteller should tell the listeners that their participation is an important part of the story and encourage them to listen and observe; so they will be ready to participate when it is time do so. Then he tells the listeners exactly what he wants them to do. Three steps are helpful in informing the audience how to participate.

1st **Describe the audience participation action**

Tell the audience what you want them to do; then model the action. The younger the children, the more explicit the instruction needs to be.

2nd **Inform the listeners about the signal for participation**

Describe and show the signal for the listeners to start participation. The clearest signal is a physical gesture, such as extending both hands, palms up, and fingers spread toward the listeners.

3rd **Rehearse**

The storyteller should invite the listeners to practice the audience participation action with him once or twice.

Audience participation increases the joy of storytelling for both the teller and the listeners. The storyteller should craft some stories that invite the audience to participate.

Story Crafting

CATEGORIES OF STORIES

1. A **myth** is a traditional story that is not true in a literal sense, but serves to explain people's world-view, an event in nature or a specific belief or culture. A myth is usually a story about the early history of a distinct people group and explains a natural or social phenomenon. Typically, it involves the supernatural. Myths often deal with gods shaped in the image of people and are influenced by humanity's questioning of the mysteries of life and the infinite.

2. A **fairy tale (wonder story)** is a story about magical beings, such as a fairies, giants, dwarfs, and animals that talk. Some storytellers call them **wonder stories** since not all are about fairies.

3. A **folktale** is a tale circulated by word of mouth among the common people. It is a traditional story of unknown authorship that is transmitted orally. Every country and people group has its folktales.

4. A **folktale variant** is a different version of a familiar story that comes from other countries or cultures. Hundreds of versions exist of "Cinderella" and "Jack and the Beanstalk."

5. A **ballad** is a song that tells a popular story. Many folktales were put to song and became ballads.

6. A **legend** is a traditional story popularly regarded as historical but which is not authenticated. Legends are about people, places or events that have some basis in historical facts; however, the stories have been retold so often and the happenings have

Story Crafting

been exaggerated to such an extent that it is impossible to prove what exactly happened. Examples include tales about King Arthur, Robin Hood, David Crockett or Daniel Boone.

7. A **local legend** is a traditional popular story based on people and events in the local geographic area.

8. A **contemporary legend** (often called an **urban legend**) is a made up or an exaggerated story that is told as a true, recent happening. The teller may believe it true. He creates credibility by establishing a relationship to the people involved in the story, such as saying it happened to a friend of a friend, and naming the location where the event happened.

9. A **Native American tale** is a story told within an Indian tribe in North America.

10. A **fantasy story** is an interesting but highly implausible story. Make-believe, talking animals and inanimate objects are involved in a fantasy story. The story usually includes magic, an enchantment or other supernatural elements that are clearly imaginary and would be impossible in the real world.

11. A **science fiction story** is a form of fantasy. It has unreal elements that are based on scientific possibilities. The story is usually set in the future.

12. A **fable** is a short, moral story about mythical or supernatural beings, things, events or animals. In most cases it is a story in which the main characters are animals who are behaving like people. It always teaches a moral lesson, which is usually clearly stated at the end.

13. An **animal tale** uses animals as the main characters. In most cases it is a story in which the main characters are animals who are behaving like people.

14. A **nursery story** is a story for very young children. It is usually found in a book that was written to be read to little children.

Categories of Stories

15. A **riddle story** presents a difficult problem or mystery that requires ingenuity in finding its answer or meaning, and the audience is invited to solve it before the answer is told.

16. An **adventure story** is one in which the key-character(s) must overcome great obstacles. He usually has a task to complete or a goal to reach. The story is usually filled with fast-moving action and with frequent location changes

17. A **trickster tale** is about a troublemaker who cheats or deceives people. He gets into mischief by playing tricks on others. Often the trick is on the trickster. The trickster is usually male and has a dual personality. In some stories he is a hero; in others he is a scoundrel; he may even be both in the same story.

18. A **how and why story** answers questions that explain the origin of certain characteristics of animals, nature, people groups, natural geological formations or some scientific phenomena.

19. A **triumphant tale** tells the story about the weaker or smaller character who achieves victory through wisdom or cleverness.

20. A **ghost or scary story** is a tale of death, murder, revenge or the spirit of a dead person. It involves supernatural elements. The story may be completely imaginary or adapted from historical facts. Scary stories often end with a "jump" that startles the audience. Different categories of ghost stories exist, such as haunted places, protective spirits, omens of death, hidden treasure, revenge sought by murdered people, ghostly animals, and weird creatures.

21. An **anecdote** is a short story that makes or illustrates a point. It may be a factual or a witty story, but it moves directly toward its goal. It economizes words to get to the point quickly and to make the point clear and unmistakable.

22. A **humorous story** is told for the purpose of evoking pleasure in the listeners by getting them to laugh. The humorous story may be a long story that wanders around and arrives nowhere

Story Crafting

in particular. Usually the teller tells the story in a quite sedated manner, and conceals the fact that he even suspects that anything is funny about it.

23. A **literary story** is a copyrighted written story that an author has published using his imagination. It is usually valued for quality of form.

24. A **circular tale** starts and ends with the same situation. The story starts with an initial-situation. Sequences of events are added to the story until it comes full circle, making the final-situation the same as the initial-situation.

25. A **cumulative tale** keeps adding sequence of events, characters, activities or situations to a tale, until a surprise occurs in the final-situation. Each time something is added, the entire list of things that preceded is recited until the newest item is tagged onto the list. (Often the list is recited backward.) The final item tagged to the story is a surprise that concludes the story.

26. A **historical story** tells about true events that happened to real people in past years.

27. **Historical fiction** is a crafted story based on a historical event. The time and place of the story are real and portrayed authentically. Also, some of the characters may be real people. Historical fiction may portray true people in imaginary situations or imaginary people in historical settings.

28. A **fiction story** is crafted, using the imagination. The storyteller creates fiction by inventing people and situations.

29. The **non-fiction crafted story** blends facts and fiction. The story is based on facts; however, the storyteller uses his imagination to reinvent the situation, to create dialogue and to fill in unavailable facts. Facts that can be verified are used. Facts are invented to fill in incomplete knowledge or faded memory. Facts may be adapted to make it a better story. Several real problems that different real people faced can be adapted so that one character faces them all.

30. A **mystery story** is filled with suspense and contains a problem or crime to solve. The sequence of events contains clues that lead the key-character to the solution. The mystery story usually contains the key-character doing the detective work, a victim, a wrongdoer, and other suspects who are found out to be innocent. Surprises add to the suspense in a mystery story.

31. A **personal story** grows out of a storyteller's own experiences. They are based on true experiences of the storyteller. A personal story may be literal truth, or it may tell about events which have been embellished and rearranged for the sake of a story. The story may be either humorous or serious.

32. A **testimony** is an honest account of personal experiences, narrated in such a way that it gives meaning to the people, events, emotional responses, and experiences in the person's life. A testimony should be the truth and nothing but the truth.

33. A **parable** is a crafted story with a moral. It is not a true story; however, its purpose is to communicate a truth. Many parables are crafted for the purpose of communicating divine truth.

34. A **Bible story** is a narrative found in the Scripture. Almost 70% of the Bible is in story form.

Story Crafting

SUGGESTED READING

FINDING STORIES TO TELL IN YOUR LIBRARY

Here is information on the Dewey Decimal numbers to help you find stories in your public library. Your library may use different numbering, so if you can't find something, ask your librarians for help.

027	This section has books about libraries for children. Some storytelling resources can be found.
133.1	Ghost, haunting, and horror stories
292	Greek and Roman mythology
272.642	Books about elementary education. Some books on storytelling
372	Reading education. Some books on storytelling
398s	**Folklore. This is where you will find the most stories to tell.**
398.2	Folktales, fairy tales and other narratives
398.6	Riddles
398.8	Rhymes
398.9	Proverbs
649.58	Books on child rearing. Some books on storytelling

782.1	Opera. Has books with plots/stories told in operas
792.8	Ballet. Has books with plots/stories told in ballets
808.5	Books on public speaking. Has some books on storytelling
808.87-.88	Toasts, jokes and stories for public speakers
810	American literature
817 818	These sections include diverse literary offerings that include short stories and collections of humor.
823	English literature
920s	Biographies. Biographies are arranged by the last name of the person whose life is the subject of the biography
B-O-ED	Recordings of books and stories

BOOKS ON STORYTELLING

Buckley, Ray. <u>Dancing with Words</u>. Nashville: Discipleship Resources, 2003

Collins, Rives; Cooper, Pamela. <u>The Power of Story; Teaching through Storytelling</u>. Long Grove, Illinois: Waveland Press, Inc., 2005

* Davis, Donald. <u>Telling Your Own Stories</u>. Little Rock: August House, 1993

___ <u>Writing as a Second Language</u>. Little Rock: August House, 2000

Egan, Kieran. <u>Teaching as Story Telling</u>. Chicago: University of Chicago Press, 1989

Geisler, Harlynne. <u>Storytelling Professionally</u>. Englewood: Libraries Unlimited, Inc., 1997

Gillard, Marni. <u>Storyteller Storyteacher: Discovering the Power of Storytelling for Teaching and Living</u>. York, Maine: Stenhouse Publishers, 1996

Haven, Kendall; Ducey, MaryGay. <u>Crash Course in Storytelling</u>. Westport, CT: Libraries Unlimited, 2007

* Haven, Kendal. <u>Write Right, Creative Writing Using Storytelling Techniques</u>. Englewood, Colorado: Teachers Ideas Press, 1999

* Lipman, Doug. <u>Improving Your Storytelling</u>. Little Rock: August House, 1999

MacDonald, Margaret Read. <u>The Storyteller's Start-Up Book</u>. Little Rock: August House, 1993

Maguire, Jack. <u>Creative Storytelling. Choosing, Inventing, and Sharing Tales for Children</u>. Cambridge, Massachusetts, Mc Graw Hill, 1985

Mellon, Nancy. <u>Storytelling and the Art of Imagination</u>. Cambridge, Massachusetts: Yellow Moon Press, 1992

* Mooney, Bill; Holts, David, editors. <u>The Storyteller's Guide</u>. Little Rock: August House, 1996

Suggested Reading

Moore, Robin, <u>Creating a Family Storytelling Tradition</u>. Little Rock: August House, 1991

Rydell, Katy. <u>A Beginner's Guide to Storytelling</u>. Jonesborough, TN: National Storytelling Press, 2003

* Simmons, Annette, <u>The Story Factor</u>. New York: Basic Books, 2002

Walsh, John. <u>The Art of Storytelling</u>. Moody Press, 2003

ATTENTION: August House Publishers, Inc. specializes in books on storytelling. <www.augusthouse.com> (800) 284-8784

* Most recommended

www.ingramcontent.com/pod-product-compliance
Lightning Source LLC
Chambersburg PA
CBHW050649160426
43194CB00010B/1864